40

With Jesus

A Journey through Mark's Gospel

Mission Co-ordinator:

Dominic

Smart

BOOT CAMP

READ

LEARN

THINK

PRAY

BOOT CAMP

READ

LEARN

THINK

PRAY

BLYTHSWOOD CARE

CHRISTIAN FOCUS

© Blythswood Care 2006

ISBN 978-1-84550-193-8

Published by Christian Focus Publications

Geanies House, Fearn, Tain, Ross-shire,

IV20 1TW, Scotland, UK.

www.christianfocus.com

Think Spots; Boot Camp; Words; Who's Who

© Christian Focus Publications 2006

Cover design: Danie van Stratten

Printed and bound: CPD

The Publishers wish to express specific thanks to

Elma Ross and

James Macdonald

for their support and creative input

into this project.

CHRISTIAN FOCUS
Good Books with the Real Message of Hope

Jesus went into Galilee,
proclaiming the good news of God.
"The time has come," he said.
"The kingdom of God is near.
Repent and believe the good news!"
Mark 1:14–15.

MISSION AND TASK

For the next 40 Days your mission is to read through the Gospel of Mark and find out what God is Saying To You.

READ

SCRIPTURE READINGS
Location: Pages 10–125.
Description: Read through the Gospel of Mark.

LEARN

DAILY LESSONS
Location: Pages 10–125.
Description: What the Gospel of Mark means.

THINK

THINK SPOTS
Location: At different points throughout the book.
Description: Extra information.

PRAY

PRAYER POINTS
Location: At the end of each reading.
Description: A time of prayer and conversation with God.

RESEARCH FACILITY

Further information about words and concepts highlighted in the book.

WORDS

WORDS
Root out the meanings of certain words on pages 126–130.

WHO'S WHO

WHO'S WHO
Get introduced to the main characters on pages 131–134.

BOOT
CAMP

BOOT CAMP

If you feel ready you can start the Mission by turning straight to Page 10 and getting right into the Bible. However some of us will need a bit of help to get started so you can go over some of the basics in the Boot Camp section at the back of the book. These are lessons that can help you get to grips with some information before you start the main lessons.

Location: Page 135–141.
Description: initiation for the 40 days Task.

MAPS

See where it all took place for yourself on our Mission Maps on pages 142–143.

MAPS

Turn the page to read
the mission statement
from Dominic smart.

Your Mission — should you choose to accept it...

READ THE BOOK OF MARK IN 40 DAYS

These notes take us on a journey with the most important man in the universe, Jesus Christ. Our guide for the journey is called John Mark. John was his Jewish name, Mark was his Roman name. He was the son of a believing woman called Mary, who lived at Jerusalem: the disciples used to meet at her house. (Disciples: See Who's Who Section on Pages 131–134.) Peter, after being rescued from prison by an angel, "went to the house of Mary, mother of John, also called Mark, where many people had gathered and were praying." (Acts 12:12). He is a nephew of Barnabas (Colossians 4:10).

WHAT DID MARK DO?

Mark travelled from Jerusalem to Antioch with Paul and Barnabas on their first journey, about AD 47 (Acts 12:25), and accompanied them to other countries as their helper (Acts 13:5).

When they returned and came ashore at Perga in Pamphylia, he left them and returned to Jerusalem; we don't know why (Acts 13:13). Three years later, he would have gone with Paul and Barnabas again; but Paul refused to take him because he had left them at Perga. This was the cause of a split between Paul and Barnabas. Mark went with his Uncle Barnabas to Cyprus (Acts 15:36-41).

Yet at some later point, Paul and Mark were fully reconciled (2 Timothy 4:11 "Get Mark and bring him with you, because he is helpful to me in my ministry"). We learn the same from Philemon (verse 24), where Mark is called Paul's fellow-worker, and from Colossians 4:10, where we find Paul passing greetings from him to the Church there.

From the references to Peter in the Gospel, and because Mark's family was known to Peter, it would seem that he was particularly close to Paul; he may well have been converted through Peter's ministry. Peter calls him his "son" in 1 Peter 5:13. Mark was not an eyewitness of Jesus, and it is likely that he gained his knowledge of Jesus' life and ministry from Peter.

WHAT DID MARK WRITE?

Mark's story of Jesus is full of action. Jesus is always on the move. He is totally involved in the same busy and hurting world that you and I live in. He shows that he is God's servant-king by his miracles. He frees people from Satan's grip by casting out demons. He meets people where they live, answers their questions, teaches them the truth and loves them just as they are. As Mark takes us on the journey that Jesus took we see just how wonderful Jesus is.

Mark probably wrote his Gospel for the church in Rome while living there some time around the early 60s AD. The Christians would have been able to use it to explain to others who Jesus is, what he did, why they follow him, and why everyone should choose to follow him. His Gospel was written so that we might meet Jesus, and give our lives to him.

WHAT ABOUT YOU?

You are starting on a journey too. God wants you to make your journey through the rest of your life with Jesus – his Son, your Saviour and the Lord of the entire universe. So when you read these notes each day, ask God to help you to follow the one that you are reading about. Many, many people will be praying for you.

God bless you,

Dominic.

Mission Co-ordinator data file: Turn to Page 8.

Accept your mission: Turn to Page 9.

Get started with your mission: Turn to Page 10.

Brush up with a boot camp before you get started: Turn to Page 135–141.

Check out the maps: Turn to Pages 142–143 and find out about some of the geographic locations mentioned throughout Mark's Gospel.

MISSION CO-ORDINATOR - DOMINIC SMART.

PLACE OF BIRTH:

Dominic Smart was born in Yorkshire, but has lived in Scotland for the past twenty-five years.

PRESENT SITUATION:

He is the Minister of Gilcomston South Church in the centre of Aberdeen. He is a regular speaker at conferences and universities and is a visiting lecturer at the Highland Theological College.

FAMILY LIFE:

Dominic and his wife Marjorie have three daughters and a son. They also have a couple of pets: two cats and a Springer spaniel.

SPARE TIME:

Dominic likes jazz music, films, Indian food and proper coffee but can't get enough of any of them; the nearest thing to a hobby is trying to catch up on sleep.

CHRISTIAN LIFE:

He became a Christian in 1973 after an Arthur Blessitt meeting in Bradford City football ground, and for many years was involved in United Beach Missions. He has written several books, including *When We Get It Wrong*, on failure; *Grace, Faith and Glory*, on the Bible's antidotes to legalism; and *Kingdom Builders*, on Peter, Stephen and Philip in Acts.

STRANGE BUT TRUE:

Dominic would like to change two things about himself – everything he does and everything he says. But even then it would probably be wrong! His only really embarrassing moment was genuinely too embarrassing to tell in public.

MISSION ACCEPTED?

Yes! I want to read Mark's Gospel in the next 40 Days and find out more about Jesus Christ.

Signed:

....

Date:

....

DAY 1 MARK 1:1–8

The beginning of the Gospel about Jesus Christ, the Son of God.

² It is written in Isaiah the prophet:

"I will send my messenger ahead of you, who will prepare your way" – ³ "a voice of one calling in the desert, 'Prepare the way for the Lord, make straight paths for him.'"

⁴ And so John came, baptising in the desert region and preaching a baptism of repentance for the forgiveness of sins. ⁵ The whole Judean countryside and all the people of Jerusalem went out to him. Confessing their sins, they were baptised by him in the Jordan River. ⁶ John wore clothing made of camel's hair, with a leather belt round his waist, and he ate locusts and wild honey.

⁷ And this was his message: "After me will come one more powerful than I, the thongs of whose sandals I am not worthy to stoop down and untie. ⁸ I baptise you with water, but he will baptise you with the Holy Spirit."

GOSPEL. This is another word for good news. Think about the different kinds of good news you can get. God's good news is much better. God's good news for us is that our sins can be forgiven and that he loves us. Through Christ's death we can be saved from the punishment of sin. God sets his people free and God keeps them safe – for ever.

Words: Anointed; Baptised. Pages 126–130.
Who's Who: John the Baptist; Jesus Christ. Pages 131–134.
Boot Camp: Introducing Jesus. Pages 135–141.

DAY 1 MARK 1:1—8. GOOD NEWS ALL THE WAY.

Mark's book is good news from God. God's good news is not really about being religious; it's not about trying to be good enough. God's good news is about Jesus Christ.

Mark wants us to know, right at the start of his book, that Jesus is God. He quotes from Isaiah chapter 40, where God begins to give his people hope because of his unfailing love. Because he loves them he will send a saviour. It is Jesus who is the Christ: God's anointed King and Saviour. He is the Lord.

So we cannot ignore Jesus. We must never forget him. Mark tells of John the Baptist. John made it clear that the right response to King Jesus is first to repent so that sins might be forgiven. Before any other problems can be sorted, we have to get our sins dealt with.

READ THIS THEN PRAY:
"Wash away all my iniquity and cleanse me from my sin."
Psalm 51:2

Prayer: Lord Jesus, I know that you came because you love me and because I need you to save me from my sin. Please forgive my sin; wash it away. Thank you that you are with me on this journey through life. Amen.

DAY 2 MARK 1:9–11

[9] At that time Jesus came from Nazareth in Galilee and was baptised by John in the Jordan. [10] As Jesus was coming up out of the water, he saw heaven being torn open and the Spirit descending on him like a dove. [11] And a voice came from heaven: "You are my Son, whom I love; with you I am well pleased."

SIN. We have to have our sin dealt with. Sin is a problem. Jesus deals with the problem. One of the ways to explain how he does this is by using the word covering. He takes his goodness and covers our badness with it. When God looks at us he sees Jesus' goodness. Our sin is no longer there. All our sin is covered. This is not Jesus pretending to God the Father in order to trick him. God the Father is fully aware of what is happening. He has planned it all.

Words: Confess; Baptise; Gospel; Faithful; Father. Pages 126–130.
Who's who: God the Father; God the Son. Pages 131–134.
Boot Camp: Getting Started with God. Pages 135–141.
Maps: Nazareth; River Jordan. Pages 142–143.

DAY 2 MARK 1:9–11. BAPTISED FOR YOU.

We learn from Matthew's Gospel that baptising people in the River Jordan had to do with confessing sin and repenting of it – turning away from sin. So why was Jesus baptised? He hadn't any sins to confess so he didn't need to be forgiven. He was baptised for you. When you or I repent, we don't do it very well. Even our repentance is full of selfishness; and there might be many things that we never even think need to be forgiven. So Jesus 'did' repentance for you and for me – getting it right for us where we get it wrong. We can trust Jesus to cover all our sin: even our sinful repentance. What a wonderful Saviour! And the Father wants everyone to know that Jesus is the faithful and much loved Son, who has pleased him by his obedience. He speaks from heaven so that we might be in no doubt that Jesus is God for us.

READ THIS THEN PRAY:
"He who conceals his sins does not prosper, but whoever confesses and renounces them finds mercy." Proverbs 28:13

Prayer: Thank you, Father, that when I confess my sins you are faithful and just and will forgive my sins. Thank you that you make it clear that Jesus is more than simply a good man – he is God the Son. Help me to confess my sin and to follow Jesus today. Amen.

Got a bit of extra time? Take a look at the map feature on Pages 142–143 and keep a note of the places you visit through Mark's Gospel.

DAY 3 MARK 1:12–13

¹² At once the Spirit sent him out into the desert, ¹³ and he was in the desert for forty days, being tempted by Satan. He was with the wild animals, and angels attended him.

JESUS KNOWS. If someone gives you advice about a trip you plan to take it is quite possible that he can't really help you. He may not have done the journey for himself.

It's not like this with Jesus. He is fully human and fully God. He knows about our struggles. Jesus has walked our road – he knows what it is like to be human. Yet, because he is God he is also able to defeat sin. He did this on the cross!

REPRESENTATIVE. If a person is accused of a crime he needs someone to speak up for him or represent him in a court of law. Jesus represents those who trust in him.

He represents them to the Judge of all the earth: God. Because Jesus represents his people in heaven his people are free from the punishment of sin.

DAY 3 MARK 1:12-13. FIGHTING TEMPTATION.

Jesus was hungry, tired and alone. If Satan can get Jesus to sin – just once – he will have stopped Jesus from his mission to save even before it's begun. A vital fight is on. Jesus wins by using God's word to answer Satan – so can we; and by desiring to serve and glorify his Father more than anything else – just like we can.

But why did he have to go through this? It's because you and I are tempted. Jesus is one of us, as well as God. Because he is fully God and fully man he can speak to God the Father on our behalf. He knows how you feel when you are tempted to do wrong. He understands how weak we are. Our bodies give in to temptation easily. Our minds will often think about ungodly things and sin. He prays for you and knows what he is talking about. He can really represent you to the Father.

 READ THIS THEN PRAY:
"For we do not have a high priest who is unable to sympathize with our weaknesses, but we have one who has been tempted in every way, just as we are – yet was without sin. Let us then approach the throne of grace with confidence, so that we may receive mercy and find grace to help us in our time of need." Hebrews 4:15–16

Prayer: Thank you Lord Jesus that you know about my struggles and problems. You are human. You understand what it is to be human. Thank you Lord Jesus that because you are also fully God you can help me. I can come to you with complete confidence in you and your love. Amen.

Words: Temptation; Glorify. Pages 126–130.
Who's who: Matthew; Satan. Pages 131–134.

DAY 4 MARK 1:14–45

14 After John was put in prison, Jesus went into Galilee, proclaiming the good news of God. 15 "The time has come," he said. "The kingdom of God is near. Repent and believe the good news!"

16 As Jesus walked beside the Sea of Galilee, he saw Simon and his brother Andrew casting a net into the lake, for they were fishermen. 17 "Come, follow me," Jesus said, "and I will make you fishers of men."

18 At once they left their nets and followed him. 19 When he had gone a little farther, he saw James son of Zebedee and his brother John in a boat, preparing their nets. 20 Without delay he called them, and they left their father Zebedee in the boat with the hired men and followed him.

21 They went to Capernaum, and when the Sabbath came, Jesus went into the synagogue and began to teach. 22 The people were amazed at his teaching, because he taught them as one who had authority, not as the teachers of the law. 23 Just then a man in their synagogue who was possessed by an evil spirit cried out, 24 "What do you want with us, Jesus of Nazareth? Have you come to destroy us? I know who you are – the Holy One of God!"

25 "Be quiet!" said Jesus sternly. "Come out of him!" 26 The evil spirit shook the man violently and came out of him with a shriek.

27 The people were all so amazed that they asked each other, "What is this? A new teaching – and with authority! He even gives orders to evil spirits and they obey him." 28 News about him spread quickly over the whole region of Galilee.

29 As soon as they left the synagogue, they went with James and John to the home of Simon and Andrew. 30 Simon's mother-in-law was in bed with a fever, and they told Jesus about her. 31 So he went to her, took her hand and helped her up. The fever left her and she began to wait on them. 32 That evening after sunset the people brought to Jesus all the sick and demon-possessed. 33 The whole town gathered at the door, 34 and Jesus healed many who had various diseases. He also drove out many demons, but he would not let the demons speak because they knew who he was.

35 Very early in the morning, while it was still dark, Jesus got up, left the house and went off to a solitary place, where he prayed. 36 Simon and his companions went to look for him, 37 and when they found him, they exclaimed: "Everyone is looking for you!"

38 Jesus replied, "Let us go somewhere else – to the nearby villages – so that I can preach there also. That is why I have come." 39 So he travelled throughout Galilee, preaching in their synagogues and driving out demons.

40 A man with leprosy came to him and begged him on his knees, "If you are willing, you can make me clean."

41 Filled with compassion, Jesus reached out his hand and touched the man. "I am willing," he said. "Be clean!"

42 Immediately the leprosy left him and he was cured. 43 Jesus sent him away at once with a strong warning: 44 "See that you don't tell this to anyone. But go, show yourself to the priest and offer the sacrifices that Moses commanded for your cleansing, as a testimony to them." 45 Instead he went out and began to talk freely, spreading the news. As a result, Jesus could no longer enter a town openly but stayed outside in lonely places. Yet the people still came to him from everywhere.

TURN OVER PAGE FOR THE DEVOTIONAL AND THINK SECTIONS.

DAY 4 MARK 1:14–45. THE KING'S ENTRANCE.

It's a longer reading today but it's so important. Jesus teaches with authority. He shows authority over demons. He rules over sickness. He is full of compassion and people felt that they could bring their problems to him. Now here's the thing for you: this kind King who rules all things says to you exactly what he said to the fishermen. "Come, follow me, and I will make you fishers of men." Will you follow him and will you win people for Jesus? What's your answer? Make it 'Yes'.

FISHING FOR MEN. Those who have trusted in Jesus Christ to save them from sin want to obey him because they love him. They love him because he first loved them. If you love the Lord Jesus Christ you will want others to love him too. You know that they need to be saved from sin. You know how wonderful Jesus is and that all should love him. When you tell others about your wonderful Saviour that is what it is like to be a 'fisher of men'. You are telling others about Jesus so that they will come to Jesus and be saved. First trust in Jesus, then tell others.

PRAYER. Prayer is when we talk with God. It is communicating with him. When we pray to God we can tell him that we love him and that we are sorry for our sins. We can thank him for being such a wonderful God and for all the wonderful things he has done for us. These are all important parts of prayer, as well as asking God for the things that we need. God can provide for our daily needs and our spiritual needs. He can supply us with all our needs.

READ THIS THEN PRAY:
"Teach me, O LORD, to follow your decrees; then I will keep them to the end." Psalm 119:33

Prayer: Jesus I will follow you for the rest of my life. I will look for ways to help other people follow you too. Thank you that you want me to follow you. Amen.

DAY 5 MARK 2:1−12

A few days later, when Jesus again entered Capernaum, the people heard that he had come home. 2 So many gathered that there was no room left, not even outside the door, and he preached the word to them. 3 Some men came, bringing to him a paralytic, carried by four of them. 4 Since they could not get him to Jesus because of the crowd, they made an opening in the roof above Jesus and, after digging through it, lowered the mat the paralysed man was lying on. 5 When Jesus saw their faith, he said to the paralytic, "Son, your sins are forgiven."

6 Now some teachers of the law were sitting there, thinking to themselves, 7 "Why does this fellow talk like that? He's blaspheming! Who can forgive sins but God alone?"

8 Immediately Jesus knew in his spirit that this was what they were thinking in their hearts, and he said to them, "Why are you thinking these things? 9 Which is easier: to say to the paralytic, 'Your sins are forgiven,' or to say, 'Get up, take your mat and walk'? 10 But that you may know that the Son of Man has authority on earth to forgive sins...." He said to the paralytic, 11 "I tell you, get up, take your mat and go home." 12 He got up, took his mat and walked out in full view of them all. This amazed everyone and they praised God, saying, "We have never seen anything like this!"

FAITH IN JESUS. The Bible says "Faith is being sure of what we hope for and certain of what we do not see." (Hebrews 11:1). You might hope to get good test results, but that hope depends on how hard you work. If you believe in Jesus you have a hope that you are saved from your sin. This hope is different. Jesus is utterly dependable. This hope is sure and certain. A Christian's hope of heaven is a fact because Jesus has done everything necessary to make it true.

DAY 5 MARK 2:1–12. THE KING'S CONFLICT – PART 1.

In this story, Jesus begins to make enemies. The man who cannot walk and everyone else in the packed room expect a healing miracle. They do get one: the man does get to walk. But it's not what he needed most. Even though he had everyone's sympathy, and wouldn't have seemed like a really bad man, his most life-threatening condition was his sin, so his greatest need was to be forgiven. But everyone, especially the Teachers of the Law of Moses and the Pharisees, the religious law-enforcers, knew that only God can forgive sins. So when Jesus says "Your sins are forgiven" he makes it really clear that he claims to be God.

The Pharisees wouldn't accept that. They used their religion as a barrier to believing in Jesus. Their pride and self-righteousness made them hate Jesus.

If you follow Jesus, you will find that some people turn against you too. And if you become a 'fisher of men' you'll find many people who say that Jesus isn't who he claims to be and that they don't need Jesus.

But there will be others who will believe and praise God for Jesus, like many of the people in that crowded house.

 READ THIS THEN PRAY:
"Blessed are they whose transgressions are forgiven, whose sins are covered." Romans 4:7

Prayer: Lord, help me to remember that the deepest need of all the people that I meet today is to be forgiven. Amen.

Words: Miracle; Self-righteousness; Believe; Praise; Forgiven. Pages 126–130.
Who's Who: Pharisees. Pages 131–134.

DAY 6 MARK 2:13–3:6

13 Once again Jesus went out beside the lake. A large crowd came to him, and he began to teach them. 14 As he walked along, he saw Levi son of Alphaeus sitting at the tax collector's booth. "Follow me," Jesus told him, and Levi got up and followed him. 15 While Jesus was having dinner at Levi's house, many tax collectors and "sinners" were eating with him and his disciples, for there were many who followed him.

16 When the teachers of the law who were Pharisees saw him eating with the "sinners" and tax collectors, they asked his disciples: "Why does he eat with tax collectors and 'sinners'?"

17 On hearing this, Jesus said to them, "It is not the healthy who need a doctor, but the sick. I have not come to call the righteous, but sinners."

18 Now John's disciples and the Pharisees were fasting. Some people came and asked Jesus, "How is it that John's disciples and the disciples of the Pharisees are fasting, but yours are not?"

19 Jesus answered, "How can the guests of the bridegroom fast while he is with them? They cannot, so long as they have him with them. 20 But the time will come when the bridegroom will be taken from them, and on that day they will fast. 21 No-one sews a patch of unshrunk cloth on an old garment. If he does, the new piece will pull away from the old, making the tear worse. 22 And no-one pours new wine into old wineskins. If he does, the wine will burst the skins, and both the wine and the wineskins will be ruined. No, he pours new wine into new wineskins."

23 One Sabbath Jesus was going through the cornfields, and as his disciples walked along, they began to pick some ears of corn. 24 The Pharisees said to him, "Look, why are they doing what is unlawful on the Sabbath?" 25 He answered, "Have you never read what David did when he and his companions were hungry and in need? 26 In the days of Abiathar the high priest, he entered the house of God and ate the consecrated bread, which is lawful only for priests to eat. And he also gave some to his companions."

27 Then he said to them, "The Sabbath was made for man, not man for the Sabbath. 28 So the Son of Man is Lord even of the Sabbath."

MARK 3:1-6

Another time he went into the synagogue, and a man with a shrivelled hand was there. [2] Some of them were looking for a reason to accuse Jesus, so they watched him closely to see if he would heal him on the Sabbath. [3] Jesus said to the man with the shrivelled hand, "Stand up in front of everyone."

[4] Then Jesus asked them, "Which is lawful on the Sabbath: to do good or to do evil, to save life or to kill?" But they remained silent.

[5] He looked round at them in anger and, deeply distressed at their stubborn hearts, said to the man, "Stretch out your hand." He stretched it out, and his hand was completely restored. [6] Then the Pharisees went out and began to plot with the Herodians how they might kill Jesus.

TURN OVER PAGE FOR THE DEVOTIONAL AND THINK SECTIONS.

DAY 6 MARK 2:13–3:6. THE KING'S CONFLICT – PART 2.

Jesus' enemies got even angrier. He had already claimed authority to forgive sins; here he told the Pharisees 'God loves sinners'. The Pharisees despised sinners and tax collectors (who worked with the hated Romans). Jesus said that it is right to be joyful with Jesus. The Pharisees had no real joy in God. Jesus said that they are not the way the future of God's work is going and then he told them that they didn't actually understand the Old Testament at all! Jesus was very courageous. He was on a mission to save sinners. He would not be put off by the devil or by those who rejected him.

WHAT IS FASTING? This was an important religious activity in Jesus' day. It was a time when people would stop eating food and instead they would spend time in prayer to God. When they fasted and prayed it was a serious and solemn activity.

Words: Righteous; Sabbath; House of God. Pages 126–130.
Who's Who: Levi; Tax Collectors; Disciples; John's Disciples; David; Abiathar the High Priest; Son of Man; Lord of the Sabbath; Herodians. Pages 131–134.
Boot Camp: Introducing Jesus – Authority. Pages 135–141.

WHY JESUS' DISCIPLES DIDN'T FAST. Jesus' disciples didn't need to fast because they were with God's Son himself. They had reason to be joyful and not to be sad and solemn. Jesus used the description of a wedding feast to explain this. When the bridegroom arrives it is time to rejoice. In the same way Jesus' disciples were to rejoice because he was with them. Jesus has promised to be with his people always and never to forsake them. So all who believe in him should be rejoicing!

 READ THIS THEN PRAY:
"Remember the words I spoke to you: 'No servant is greater than his master.' If they persecuted me, they will persecute you also. If they obeyed my teaching, they will obey yours also." John 15:20.

Prayer: Lord, give me courage to keep following Jesus, even if it means opposition. Amen.

DAY 7 MARK 3:7–35

⁷ Jesus withdrew with his disciples to the lake, and a large crowd from Galilee followed. ⁸ When they heard all he was doing, many people came to him from Judea, Jerusalem, Idumea, and the regions across the Jordan and around Tyre and Sidon. ⁹ Because of the crowd he told his disciples to have a small boat ready for him, to keep the people from crowding him. ¹⁰ For he had healed many, so that those with diseases were pushing forward to touch him. ¹¹ Whenever the evil spirits saw him, they fell down before him and cried out, "You are the Son of God." ¹² But he gave them strict orders not to tell who he was.

¹³ Jesus went up on a mountainside and called to him those he wanted, and they came to him. ¹⁴ He appointed twelve –designating them apostles – that they might be with him and that he might send them out to preach ¹⁵ and to have authority to drive out demons. ¹⁶ These are the twelve he appointed: Simon (to whom he gave the name Peter); ¹⁷ James son of Zebedee and his brother John (to them he gave the name Boanerges, which means Sons of Thunder); ¹⁸ Andrew, Philip, Bartholomew, Matthew, Thomas, James son of Alphaeus, Thaddaeus, Simon the Zealot ¹⁹ and Judas Iscariot, who betrayed him.

²⁰ Then Jesus entered a house, and again a crowd gathered, so that he and his disciples were not even able to eat. ²¹ When his family heard about this, they went to take charge of him, for they said, "He is out of his mind."

²² And the teachers of the law who came down from Jerusalem said, "He is possessed by Beelzebub! By the prince of demons he is driving out demons."

²³ So Jesus called them and spoke to them in parables: "How can Satan drive out Satan? ²⁴ If a kingdom is divided against itself, that kingdom cannot stand. ²⁵ If a house is divided against itself, that house cannot stand. ²⁶ And if Satan opposes himself and is divided, he cannot stand; his end has come. ²⁷ In fact, no-one can enter a strong man's house and carry off his possessions unless he first ties up the strong man. Then he can rob his house. ²⁸ I tell you the truth, all the sins and blasphemies of men will be forgiven

them. [29] But whoever blasphemes against the Holy Spirit will never be forgiven; he is guilty of an eternal sin."

[30] He said this because they were saying, "He has an evil spirit."

[31] Then Jesus' mother and brothers arrived. Standing outside, they sent someone in to call him. [32] A crowd was sitting around him, and they told him, "Your mother and brothers are outside looking for you."

[33] "Who are my mother and my brothers?" he asked.

[34] Then he looked at those seated in a circle around him and said, "Here are my mother and my brothers! [35] Whoever does God's will is my brother and sister and mother."

TURN OVER PAGE FOR THE DEVOTIONAL AND THINK SECTIONS.

DAY 7 MARK 3:7–35. THE KING'S CALL.

How talented and holy do you think the twelve were in this story? Were they all one type of person? Were they all special people? King Jesus called those who were weak, those who were sinners. He wanted their company, even though they understood so little of what he was doing. He would teach and train them, and set them an example. He was going to turn the world upside down through them. You don't have to be an outstanding Christian for Jesus to use you, or change you – you just need to listen to his call to share in his work in this needy world. It's a call to you – specifically to you. He knows your name, just like he knew theirs. He knows your weakness, just like he knew theirs. Say 'Yes' to his call to build his Kingdom with him.

KINGDOM. Jesus is described as the King of Kings. All Kings have kingdoms that they rule over. God has a kingdom. He rules earth and heaven; the universe is under his command. But when we talk about God building his kingdom what we mean is that God is bringing people into his family. God's kingdom is made up of people who love and trust in him. When we build God's kingdom we are working to make sure that other people know about the good news that Jesus saves sinners.

LOST. There are always two types of people with Jesus – people who believe in him and people who don't. If you believe in him you are a Christian and you are part of God's family. If you don't believe in Jesus then you are not part of God's family. You are, in fact lost. Even if you go to church and read your Bible you can still be a lost sinner instead of a saved sinner, if you haven't trusted in Jesus Christ.

READ THIS THEN PRAY:
"Know that the LORD has set apart the godly for himself; the LORD will hear when I call to him." Psalm 4:3

Prayer: Thank you Lord that you know me and want to change this world through me and all who say 'Yes' to your call. Use me today and every day. Amen.

DAY 8 MARK 4:1–34

Again Jesus began to teach by the lake. The crowd that gathered round him was so large that he got into a boat and sat in it out on the lake, while all the people were along the shore at the water's edge. ² He taught them many things by parables, and in his teaching said: ³ "Listen! A farmer went out to sow his seed. ⁴ As he was scattering the seed, some fell along the path, and the birds came and ate it up. ⁵ Some fell on rocky places, where it did not have much soil. It sprang up quickly, because the soil was shallow. ⁶ But when the sun came up, the plants were scorched, and they withered because they had no root. ⁷ Other seed fell among thorns, which grew up and choked the plants, so that they did not bear grain. ⁸ Still other seed fell on good soil. It came up, grew and produced a crop, multiplying thirty, sixty, or even a hundred times."

⁹ Then Jesus said, "He who has ears to hear, let him hear."

¹⁰ When he was alone, the Twelve and the others around him asked him about the parables. ¹¹ He told them, "The secret of the kingdom of God has been given to you. But to those on the outside everything is said in parables ¹² so that, 'they may be ever seeing but never perceiving, and ever hearing but never understanding; otherwise they might turn and be forgiven!'"

¹³ Then Jesus said to them, "Don't you understand this parable? How then will you understand any parable? ¹⁴ The farmer sows the word. ¹⁵ Some people are like seed along the path, where the word is sown. As soon as they hear it, Satan comes and takes away the word that was sown in them. ¹⁶ Others, like seed sown on rocky places, hear the word and at once receive it with joy. ¹⁷ But since they have no root, they last only a short time. When trouble or persecution comes because of the word, they quickly fall away. ¹⁸ Still others, like seed sown among thorns, hear the word; ¹⁹ but the worries of this life, the deceitfulness of wealth and the desires for other things come in and choke the word, making it unfruitful. ²⁰ Others, like seed sown on good soil, hear the word, accept it, and produce a crop – thirty, sixty or even a hundred times what was sown."

[21] He said to them, "Do you bring in a lamp to put it under a bowl or a bed? Instead, don't you put it on its stand? [22] For whatever is hidden is meant to be disclosed, and whatever is concealed is meant to be brought out into the open. [23] If anyone has ears to hear, let him hear."

[24] "Consider carefully what you hear," he continued. "With the measure you use, it will be measured to you - and even more. [25] Whoever has will be given more; whoever does not have, even what he has will be taken from him."

[26] He also said, "This is what the kingdom of God is like. A man scatters seed on the ground. [27] Night and day, whether he sleeps or gets up, the seed sprouts and grows, though he does not know how. [28] All by itself the soil produces corn – first the stalk, then the ear, then the full grain in the ear. [29] As soon as the grain is ripe, he puts the sickle to it, because the harvest has come."

[30] Again he said, "What shall we say the kingdom of God is like, or what parable shall we use to describe it? [31] It is like a mustard seed, which is the smallest seed you plant in the ground. [32] Yet when planted, it grows and becomes the largest of all garden plants, with such big branches that the birds of the air can perch in its shade."

[33] With many similar parables Jesus spoke the word to them, as much as they could understand. [34] He did not say anything to them without using a parable. But when he was alone with his own disciples, he explained everything.

TURN OVER PAGE FOR THE DEVOTIONAL AND THINK SECTIONS.

DAY 8 MARK 4:1-34. THE KING'S
STORIES.

Parables are like a filter. They filter out those who have faith in Jesus and see the point, from those who don't believe and don't understand. And it's that way round. Believe and then see. Accept that Jesus is Lord and you'll see that he really is. Why should God have to prove himself to anyone? If he had to do that, they would be God, passing judgement on Jesus!

He told great stories that really stick in our minds and make us ask questions about ourselves. What kind of ground are you? Do you see Jesus as the light of the world, or do you hide him out of embarrassment? Can you wait while God does unseen work in the heart of a non-Christian friend? Do you believe that God's kingdom is going to grow and grow beyond all other earthly power?

LIGHT AND LIFE. Jesus is the light of the world. He lights up what we need to see. He shows us our sin, he shows us our need to be saved from sin, he shows us that he is the only way to be saved from sin. Sin is darkness and death. Jesus is the opposite – he is light and life.

SAVIOUR. Do you believe in Jesus as your Saviour? If you do and you have friends and family who don't it can be hard. You will long for them to come to know Jesus as their Saviour too. Pray to God that he will bring them to believe in him. But God can work in people's hearts without us knowing.

 READ THIS THEN PRAY:
"But if ... you seek the LORD your God, you will find him if you look for him with all your heart and with all your soul." Deuteronomy 4:29

Prayer: Lord, give me a heart full of faith, eyes to see your truth, and a voice to speak about you. Amen.

Words: Parable. Pages 126–130.
Boot Camp: Getting started with you. Pages 135–141.

DAY 9 MARK 4:35–41

³⁵ That day when evening came, he said to his disciples, "Let us go over to the other side." ³⁶ Leaving the crowd behind, they took him along, just as he was, in the boat. There were also other boats with him. ³⁷ A furious squall came up, and the waves broke over the boat, so that it was nearly swamped. ³⁸ Jesus was in the stern, sleeping on a cushion. The disciples woke him and said to him, "Teacher, don't you care if we drown?"

³⁹ He got up, rebuked the wind and said to the waves, "Quiet! Be still!" Then the wind died down and it was completely calm.

⁴⁰ He said to his disciples, "Why are you so afraid? Do you still have no faith?"

⁴¹ They were terrified and asked each other, "Who is this? Even the wind and the waves obey him!"

MORALS. These are the rules that people follow in their lives. People disagree on what the right rules or morals are. But it is really quite simple. The right rules are the ones God has given us. We must follow them. But remember – because we are sinners we will find it impossible to keep God's rules perfectly. Only Jesus has done that. But he did a lot more. He lived a perfect life and he died the perfect death so that those who believe in him can have a perfect life for ever.

DAY 9 MARK 4:35–41. THE KING'S AUTHORITY.

Either Jesus is mad, or he's God. He certainly isn't just a good man. People will tell you that he's a great moral teacher, or very wise, or a good example. But great moral teachers don't give instructions to the wind and waves and expect them to obey.
Jesus is God. The wind and the waves obeyed the word of their maker. We should too. There are people who think that they've understood Jesus but who won't obey him. Some dismiss Jesus with a compliment, 'He was just a good man,' or 'He was certainly wise,' or 'I admit he was a great moral teacher.' None of this is acceptable. He wants our total worship.

One other thing. The disciples were more scared of Jesus than they had been of the storm. They got more than they'd been thinking about when they asked Jesus for help. They still had a lot to learn. Imagine asking Jesus "Don't you care?" They haven't realised yet that he's going to die for them; that's how much he cares! But Jesus keeps going with them. He will keep going with you too. Don't give up.

READ THIS THEN PRAY:
"This is love for God: to obey his commands. And his commands are not burdensome." 1 John 5:3

Prayer: Thank you Lord for being patient with me when I don't understand how great you are or how much you care about me. If winds and waves obey you, Lord Jesus, so should I. Speak to me through your word and help me by your Holy Spirit so that I do your will. Amen.

Boot Camp: Introducing Jesus - Authority. Pages 135–141.

DAY 10 MARK 5:1–20

They went across the lake to the region of the Gerasenes.
[2] When Jesus got out of the boat, a man with an evil spirit
came from the tombs to meet him. [3] This man lived in the
tombs, and no-one could bind him any more, not even with a chain. [4]
For he had often been chained hand and foot, but he tore the chains
apart and broke the irons on his feet. No-one was strong enough to
subdue him. [5] Night and day among the tombs and in the hills he
would cry out and cut himself with stones.

[6] When he saw Jesus from a distance, he ran and fell on his
knees in front of him. [7] He shouted at the top of his voice, "What do
you want with me, Jesus, Son of the Most High God? Swear to God
that you won't torture me!" [8] For Jesus had said to him, "Come out
of this man, you evil spirit!"

[9] Then Jesus asked him, "What is your name?"

"My name is Legion," he replied, "for we are many." [10] And he
begged Jesus again and again not to send them out of the area.

[11] A large herd of pigs was feeding on the nearby hillside. [12] The
demons begged Jesus, "Send us among the pigs; allow us to go into
them." [13] He gave them permission, and the evil spirits came out and
went into the pigs. The herd, about two thousand in number, rushed
down the steep bank into the lake and were drowned.

[14] Those tending the pigs ran off and reported this in the town and
countryside, and the people went out to see what had happened. [15]
When they came to Jesus, they saw the man who had been possessed
by the legion of demons, sitting there, dressed and in his right mind;
and they were afraid. [16] Those who had seen it told the people what
had happened to the demon-possessed man – and told about the
pigs as well. [17] Then the people began to plead with Jesus to leave
their region.

[18] As Jesus was getting into the boat, the man who had been
demon-possessed begged to go with him. [19] Jesus did not let him,
but said, "Go home to your family and tell them how much the Lord
has done for you, and how he has had mercy on you." [20] So the man
went away and began to tell in the Decapolis how much Jesus had
done for him. And all the people were amazed.

DAY 10 MARK 5:1–20. THE KING'S POWER.

No-one could help this man. He couldn't help himself. He was a lost cause. He harmed himself, and would have harmed others if he got the chance. He was an outcast; no-one wanted him. He was only fit for the grave, until Jesus came along. Jesus knew that the man was possessed by evil spirits, but their number was up! They recognised Jesus' power and pleaded with him. But this man's condition was important to Jesus; more important than the evil spirits and the pigs. Jesus had the power to make evil depart and to heal the man. Never forget that Jesus has the power to change your life. He has power over evil. He defeated and disarmed it on the cross. One day he will finally end it.

Two other points. The man becomes a witness: others need to know how much the Lord has done for you, too. And the people thought that the pigs – their source of income and food – were more important than the man and more important than Jesus. What are your priorities: are they the same as Christ's?

READ THIS THEN PRAY:
"Even when I am old and gray, do not forsake me, O God, till I declare your power to the next generation, your might to all who are to come." Psalm 71:18

Prayer: Lord, we have read about your power to change lives. Have mercy on me; may your victory over evil be seen in my life. Help me to tell others what you have done for me. Amen.

GLORIFY GOD. Make sure that you ask Jesus to save you then tell others about him. Jesus loves us and wants the name of God to be glorified. This is Jesus' priority – to glorify God. It should be our priority too.

Who's Who: Evil spirits; Devil; God the Son. Pages 131–134.
Maps: Gerasenes; Decapolis. Pages 142–143.

DAY 11 MARK 5:21–43

21 When Jesus had again crossed over by boat to the other side of the lake, a large crowd gathered round him while he was by the lake. 22 Then one of the synagogue rulers, named Jairus, came there. Seeing Jesus, he fell at his feet 23 and pleaded earnestly with him, "My little daughter is dying. Please come and put your hands on her so that she will be healed and live." 24 So Jesus went with him.

A large crowd followed and pressed around him. 25 And a woman was there who had been subject to bleeding for twelve years. 26 She had suffered a great deal under the care of many doctors and had spent all she had, yet instead of getting better she grew worse. 27 When she heard about Jesus, she came up behind him in the crowd and touched his cloak, 28 because she thought, "If I just touch his clothes, I will be healed." 29 Immediately her bleeding stopped and she felt in her body that she was freed from her suffering.

30 At once Jesus realised that power had gone out from him. He turned around in the crowd and asked, "Who touched my clothes?"

31 "You see the people crowding against you," his disciples answered, "and yet you can ask, 'Who touched me?'"

32 But Jesus kept looking around to see who had done it. 33 Then the woman, knowing what had happened to her, came and fell at his feet and, trembling with fear, told him the whole truth. 34 He said to her, "Daughter, your faith has healed you. Go in peace and be freed from your suffering."

35 While Jesus was still speaking, some men came from the house of Jairus, the synagogue ruler. "Your daughter is dead," they said. "Why bother the teacher any more?"

36 Ignoring what they said, Jesus told the synagogue ruler, "Don't be afraid; just believe."

37 He did not let anyone follow him except Peter, James and John the brother of James. 38 When they came to the home of the synagogue ruler, Jesus saw a commotion, with people crying and wailing loudly. 39 He went in and said to them, "Why all this

commotion and wailing? The child is not dead but asleep." [40] But they laughed at him.

After he put them all out, he took the child's father and mother and the disciples who were with him, and went in where the child was. [41] He took her by the hand and said to her, "Talitha koum!" (which means, "Little girl, I say to you, get up!").

[42] Immediately the girl stood up and walked around (she was twelve years old). At this they were completely astonished. [43] He gave strict orders not to let anyone know about this, and told them to give her something to eat.

TURN OVER PAGE FOR THE DEVOTIONAL AND THINK SECTIONS.

DAY 11 MARK 5:21–43. THE KING'S COMPASSION.

The compassion of Jesus is amazing. Jairus is in the worst place that any parent could be – watching his daughter die, and unable to do anything. But he hears that Jesus is nearby, so he falls at Jesus' feet and pleads. Jesus responds to the needs of Jairus and his daughter. He isn't too busy; he isn't too important; he isn't too tired. He feels for Jairus deeply.

Then the most awful words are spoken: "Your daughter is dead" and the messengers don't think that Jesus can do anything more. It's too late. But it isn't! Jesus has the power and the authority. We've already seen that. He also has the compassion to use them. We know that because Jesus has already shown his power, love and compassion to a woman on the way to Jairus's home. She was healed, but terrified when he searched her out. But see how understanding, gentle, full of respect and thoughtful he was with her. Being powerful is one thing, but using your power with compassion is quite another.

When you are compassionate people see a reflection of Jesus.

TWELVE YEARS. It is interesting to see that the woman with the blood disease had been sick for twelve years – exactly the same number of years as the young girl had been alive. Jesus healed both of them. He showed his power and authority over disease and death. Go to the Boot Camp Section on Pages 135–141 to find out more about the Lord Jesus Christ and his authority. On Pages 131–134 you can find out a bit more about miracles too.

JESUS LOVE. Jesus shows love and compassion to all. It doesn't matter how old or young you are. It doesn't matter who you know or don't know, or if you are rich or poor. Anyone can come to him for help. Jesus has said that if you come to him to ask to be saved from your sins you will not be turned away. You won't be rejected.

READ THIS THEN PRAY:
"Therefore, as God's chosen people, holy and dearly loved, clothe yourselves with compassion, kindness, humility, gentleness and patience." Colossians 3:12

Prayer: Lord Jesus please make me into the person that you want me to be. May all my conduct and conversation give glory and honour to you. Lord, help me to know that my actions do not save me from my sin. I have you to thank for that. It is you alone who can give Salvation to sinners. Amen.

DAY 12 MARK 6:1–29

Jesus left there and went to his home town, accompanied by his disciples. ² When the Sabbath came, he began to teach in the synagogue, and many who heard him were amazed.

"Where did this man get these things?" they asked. "What's this wisdom that has been given him, that he even does miracles! ³ Isn't this the carpenter? Isn't this Mary's son and the brother of James, Joseph, Judas and Simon? Aren't his sisters here with us?" And they took offence at him.

⁴ Jesus said to them, "Only in his home town, among his relatives and in his own house is a prophet without honour." ⁵ He could not do any miracles there, except lay his hands on a few sick people and heal them. ⁶ And he was amazed at their lack of faith.

Then Jesus went round teaching from village to village. ⁷ Calling the Twelve to him, he sent them out two by two and gave them authority over evil spirits. ⁸ These were his instructions: "Take nothing for the journey except a staff – no bread, no bag, no money in your belts. ⁹ Wear sandals but not an extra tunic. ¹⁰ Whenever you enter a house, stay there until you leave that town. ¹¹ And if any place will not welcome you or listen to you, shake the dust off your feet when you leave, as a testimony against them."

¹² They went out and preached that people should repent. ¹³ They drove out many demons and anointed many sick people with oil and healed them.

¹⁴ King Herod heard about this, for Jesus' name had become well known. Some were saying, "John the Baptist has been raised from the dead, and that is why miraculous powers are at work in him."

¹⁵ Others said, "He is Elijah."

And still others claimed, "He is a prophet, like one of the prophets of long ago."

¹⁶ But when Herod heard this, he said, "John, the man I beheaded, has been raised from the dead!"

¹⁷ For Herod himself had given orders to have John arrested, and he had him bound and put in prison. He did this because of Herodias, his brother Philip's wife, whom he had married. ¹⁸ For

John had been saying to Herod, "It is not lawful for you to have your brother's wife." [19] So Herodias nursed a grudge against John and wanted to kill him. But she was not able to, [20] because Herod feared John and protected him, knowing him to be a righteous and holy man. When Herod heard John, he was greatly puzzled; yet he liked to listen to him.

[21] Finally the opportune time came. On his birthday Herod gave a banquet for his high officials and military commanders and the leading men of Galilee. [22] When the daughter of Herodias came in and danced, she pleased Herod and his dinner guests.

The king said to the girl, "Ask me for anything you want, and I'll give it to you." [23] And he promised her with an oath, "Whatever you ask I will give you, up to half my kingdom."

[24] She went out and said to her mother, "What shall I ask for?" "The head of John the Baptist," she answered.

[25] At once the girl hurried in to the king with the request: "I want you to give me right now the head of John the Baptist on a platter."

[26] The king was greatly distressed, but because of his oaths and his dinner guests, he did not want to refuse her. [27] So he immediately sent an executioner with orders to bring John's head. The man went, beheaded John in the prison, [28] and brought back his head on a platter. He presented it to the girl, and she gave it to her mother. [29] On hearing of this, John's disciples came and took his body and laid it in a tomb.

TURN OVER PAGE FOR THE DEVOTIONAL AND THINK SECTIONS.

DAY 12 MARK 6:1–29. THE KING IS REJECTED.

Jesus is rejected in his home town of Nazareth. People think that because they saw him grow up and know his family he's no different from them. So there's no need to treat him as special. How wrong can you get? Even Jesus is amazed!

But it's not only Jesus that is rejected: his friends are too. John the Baptist spoke the truth without fear. He pressed the word of God into the immoral life of Herod. But Herod didn't want to respond by repenting. Later he was an accomplice in Jesus' death. John the Baptist was rejected by those who felt guilty such as Herodias and Herod. They didn't want their consciences stabbed by John's truthfulness.

People hate the thought of being accountable to God. Speaking the word of God, especially when it shows up those sins that people love so much, can mean that you are rejected. But better to suffer with Jesus than have an easy life without him.

ACCOUNTABLE. In a democracy you are accountable to others such as the law courts or police. They have been given authority by the government. The government has been given that authority by the people. You have to be able to answer for your behaviour and actions. We are all accountable to God. If we break God's law we must be punished. Sin deserves the punishment of death. But you can have your sins covered by Jesus Christ if you turn away from your sin and give your love and your life to him.

JUDGEMENT. Sin has to be punished. There has to be a judgement. If you believe in the Lord Jesus Christ then your sin has already been punished and dealt with by his death on the cross. If you do not believe in Christ then you are at risk of taking this punishment yourself - a punishment that will be eternal and never-ending. It is one thing to talk about God being merciful - but unless you understand that God has to give judgement as well as mercy then you do not understand the full truth. To understand salvation you must realise what you are being saved from. Christ's death has saved his people from sin and hell.

READ THIS THEN PRAY:
"Heaven and earth will pass away, but my words will never pass away." Luke 21:33

Prayer: Lord, help me to be true to your word, unafraid to speak it and willing to accept the rejection that comes from fellowship with your wonderful Son. Amen.

Words: Repent. Pages 126–130.
Who's Who: King Herod; Elijah; John the Baptist, Herodians.
Pages 131–134.
Maps: Nazareth. Pages 142–143.

DAY 13 MARK 6:30—44

30 The apostles gathered round Jesus and reported to him all they had done and taught. 31 Then, because so many people were coming and going that they did not even have a chance to eat, he said to them, "Come with me by yourselves to a quiet place and get some rest."

32 So they went away by themselves in a boat to a solitary place. 33 But many who saw them leaving recognised them and ran on foot from all the towns and got there ahead of them. 34 When Jesus landed and saw a large crowd, he had compassion on them, because they were like sheep without a shepherd. So he began teaching them many things.

35 By this time it was late in the day, so his disciples came to him. "This is a remote place," they said, "and it's already very late. 36 Send the people away so that they can go to the surrounding countryside and villages and buy themselves something to eat."

37 But he answered, "You give them something to eat."

They said to him, "That would take eight months of a man's wages! Are we to go and spend that much on bread and give it to them to eat?"

38 "How many loaves do you have?" he asked. "Go and see." When they found out, they said, "Five – and two fish."

39 Then Jesus directed them to have all the people sit down in groups on the green grass. 40 So they sat down in groups of hundreds and fifties. 41 Taking the five loaves and the two fish and looking up to heaven, he gave thanks and broke the loaves. Then he gave them to his disciples to set before the people. He also divided the two fish among them all. 42 They all ate and were satisfied, 43 and the disciples picked up twelve basketfuls of broken pieces of bread and fish. 44 The number of the men who had eaten was five thousand.

DAY 13 MARK 6:1–29. THE KING PROVIDES.

The key is in the phrase 'sheep without a shepherd'. The shepherd was the most common Old Testament picture for a King. The King was to rule on God's behalf and in his way. God protected and provided for his people; the King was to do the same. Read Psalm 23, by King David; it's about the kind of King that God is.

Jesus sees that they need a good King – they need God as their King. They need to be cared for. God loves his people. Most earthly leaders are only interested in power and there's no love for the people. So Jesus the King provides for those who are following him and listening to him. It takes a miracle which was one of the signs that God's anointed king had arrived.

He can provide the food that you need because he cares for you. He recognises when you need a King who provides. He knows what you need and he is not miserly or mean. Notice that everyone had plenty to eat! If you believe in his goodness, you'll probably see it. If you don't believe it, you probably won't see it.

READ THIS THEN PRAY:
"For the LORD is good and his love endures forever." Psalm 100:5

Prayer: Lord give me a strong faith, that hopes and truly believes in your goodness and willingness to provide all my needs. Amen.

KING. In the Bible a good king was supposed to provide for his people and protect them from enemies. He used his authority and power for the sake of his subjects. Jesus, our king, is unique. We will be happy and secure if we serve and obey him. He governs us faithfully and wants our good. He even left his kingdom for a time to live among us. He died to buy his followers a place in that kingdom to enjoy now, but especially when they leave this world at death. Then they will go to heaven to share and enjoy it with him. If Jesus is your King then you should help others, in his name, as he helps you.

DAY 14 MARK 6:45-56

⁴⁵ Immediately Jesus made his disciples get into the boat and go on ahead of him to Bethsaida, while he dismissed the crowd. ⁴⁶ After leaving them, he went up on a mountainside to pray.

⁴⁷ When evening came, the boat was in the middle of the lake, and he was alone on land. ⁴⁸ He saw the disciples straining at the oars, because the wind was against them. About the fourth watch of the night he went out to them, walking on the lake. He was about to pass by them, ⁴⁹ but when they saw him walking on the lake, they thought he was a ghost. They cried out, ⁵⁰ because they all saw him and were terrified.

Immediately he spoke to them and said, "Take courage! It is I. Don't be afraid." ⁵¹ Then he climbed into the boat with them, and the wind died down. They were completely amazed, ⁵² for they had not understood about the loaves; their hearts were hardened.

⁵³ When they had crossed over, they landed at Gennesaret and anchored there. ⁵⁴ As soon as they got out of the boat, people recognised Jesus. ⁵⁵ They ran throughout that whole region and carried the sick on mats to wherever they heard he was. ⁵⁶ And wherever he went – into villages, towns or countryside – they placed the sick in the market-places. They begged him to let them touch even the edge of his cloak, and all who touched him were healed.

FEAR. 'Do not be afraid,' is the most common command in the Bible. It is given 366 times. Once for every day of the year – and the leap year!

Words: Grace; Sovereignty. Pages 126–130.
Boot Camp: Introducing Jesus - Authority. Pages 135–141.
Maps: Bethsaida; Gennesaret. Pages 142–143.

DAY 14 MARK 6:45–56. WALKING ON WATER.

Jesus can do anything. Walking on water is not a problem, but there's more to this story than the supernatural power, or else Jesus would just be showing off.

He certainly felt sorry for the disciples. They understood so little – even the feeding of the five thousand was lost on them. Like the rest, they thought that it was about food; their hearts were 'hardened' to the fact that Jesus was God and the King of kings. So their minds couldn't understand him either.

They perhaps wondered why they were struggling away in a boat and yet Jesus had not gone with them. They certainly didn't think that Jesus could walk out to catch up with them in the middle of the lake: it was more likely to them that they saw a ghost.

Yet Jesus calmly walked out to them and told them not to be afraid, but when he's in the boat the wind dies down. Just being with him stills their troubled waters.

You have to marvel at not just who Jesus is, but what Jesus is. Would you or I have been any quicker to understand than the disciples? Would we have so easily thrown overboard everything that we'd been taught about life and, in this case, lakes?

READ THIS THEN PRAY:
"Fear not, for I have redeemed you; I have summoned you by name; you are mine." Isaiah 43:1

Prayer: Lord I really don't understand what you're doing with me. Please help me to trust you with my life. Help me to believe that you can do anything that you want. May I not be afraid today. Amen.

DAY 15 MARK 7:1–23

The Pharisees and some of the teachers of the law who had come from Jerusalem gathered round Jesus and 2 saw some of his disciples eating food with hands that were "unclean", that is, unwashed. 3 (The Pharisees and all the Jews do not eat unless they give their hands a ceremonial washing, holding to the tradition of the elders. 4 When they come from the market-place they do not eat unless they wash. And they observe many other traditions, such as the washing of cups, pitchers and kettles.)

5 So the Pharisees and teachers of the law asked Jesus, "Why don't your disciples live according to the tradition of the elders instead of eating their food with 'unclean' hands?"

6 He replied, "Isaiah was right when he prophesied about you hypocrites; as it is written: 'These people honour me with their lips, but their hearts are far from me. 7 They worship me in vain; their teachings are but rules taught by men.' 8 You have let go of the commands of God and are holding on to the traditions of men."

9 And he said to them: "You have a fine way of setting aside the commands of God in order to observe your own traditions! 10 For Moses said, 'Honour your father and your mother,' and, 'Anyone who curses his father or mother must be put to death.' 11 But you say that if a man says to his father or mother: 'Whatever help you might otherwise have received from me is Corban' (that is, a gift devoted to God), 12 then you no longer let him do anything for his father or mother. 13 Thus you nullify the word of God by your tradition that you have handed down. And you do many things like that."

14 Again Jesus called the crowd to him and said, "Listen to me, everyone, and understand this. 15 Nothing outside a man can make him 'unclean' by going into him. Rather, it is what comes out of a man that makes him 'unclean'." 17 After he had left the crowd and entered the house, his disciples asked him about this parable.

18 "Are you so dull?" he asked. "Don't you see that nothing that enters a man from the outside can make him 'unclean'? 19 For it doesn't go into his heart but into his stomach, and then out of his body." (In saying this, Jesus declared all foods "clean".)

[20] He went on: "What comes out of a man is what makes him 'unclean'. [21] For from within, out of men's hearts, come evil thoughts, sexual immorality, theft, murder, adultery, [22] greed, malice, deceit, lewdness, envy, slander, arrogance and folly. [23] All these evils come from inside and make a man 'unclean'."

TURN OVER PAGE FOR THE DEVOTIONAL AND THINK SECTIONS.

DAY 15 MARK 7:1–23. THE KING AND YOUR HEART.

Jesus says that it's not what you take in that makes you unclean before God. It's what comes from your heart. Being right with God is not a matter of doing the traditional ceremonies that any religious tradition tells us to do. It's much deeper than that. Only when your heart is clean will you be clean before God. And you don't become unclean by not performing the traditional religious duties. Again, it's much deeper than that – much more challenging. Eating food that the religious traditions condemned didn't separate you from God – it's only food! 'Clean' and 'unclean' have to do with what's on the inside. The Pharisees chose to leave the heart unexamined and preferred their religious traditions to God's word.

Jesus knows us pretty well, eh? He knows what goes on in your heart. No amount of religious observance can make it clean.

So what will make us clean? Only a change of heart. Who can give us a clean heart? Only God.

How's your heart before God today? You can look very religious on the outside, but be full of evil in your heart.

 GUILTY AS CHARGED. How can I be saved from sin? No matter how many religious things you do – none of your words or actions will save you from the guilt of sin. You are guilty as charged. You can only be freed from the guilt and power of sin when you turn to the Lord Jesus Christ and ask him to save you. It is what Jesus Christ has done on the cross that saves sinners.

WHAT DID JESUS DO ON THE CROSS? You're going to find out much more about that in the coming days and weeks, but this is what happened: Jesus was put to death. He was accused falsely and nailed to a wooden cross. This was the Roman method of execution. The religious leaders and the Romans and Pilate can be accused of causing his death - but Jesus died willingly. His death was God's plan to save sinners. His death meant that eternal life could be given freely by God to those who believed in his Son, Jesus.

READ THIS THEN PRAY:
"The LORD does not look at the things man looks at. Man looks at the outward appearance, but the LORD looks at the heart." 1 Samuel 16:7

Prayer: Lord I have a sinful and impure heart. Even my good actions can have bad motives. I am a sinner through and through. Only you can clean me where it really matters. Only you can save me from sin. Please change my heart. Amen.

Words: Jews; Parable; Immorality; Adultery. Pages 126–130.
Who's Who: Isaiah; Pharisees; Moses. Pages 131–134.
Boot Camp: Getting started with you - sin. Pages 135–141.

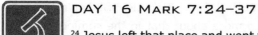

DAY 16 MARK 7:24-37

[24] Jesus left that place and went to the vicinity of Tyre. He entered a house and did not want anyone to know it; yet he could not keep his presence secret. [25] In fact, as soon as she heard about him, a woman whose little daughter was possessed by an evil spirit came and fell at his feet. [26] The woman was a Greek, born in Syrian Phoenicia. She begged Jesus to drive the demon out of her daughter.

[27] "First let the children eat all they want," he told her, "for it is not right to take the children's bread and toss it to their dogs."

[28] "Yes, Lord," she replied, "but even the dogs under the table eat the children's crumbs."

[29] Then he told her, "For such a reply, you may go; the demon has left your daughter."

[30] She went home and found her child lying on the bed, and the demon gone.

[31] Then Jesus left the vicinity of Tyre and went through Sidon, down to the Sea of Galilee and into the region of the Decapolis. [32] There some people brought to him a man who was deaf and could hardly talk, and they begged him to place his hand on the man.

[33] After he took him aside, away from the crowd, Jesus put his fingers into the man's ears. Then he spat and touched the man's tongue. [34] He looked up to heaven and with a deep sigh said to him, "Ephphatha!" (which means, "Be opened!"). [35] At this, the man's ears were opened, his tongue was loosened and he began to speak plainly.

[36] Jesus commanded them not to tell anyone. But the more he did so, the more they kept talking about it. [37] People were overwhelmed with amazement. "He has done everything well," they said. "He even makes the deaf hear and the mute speak."

DAY 16 MARK 7:24–37. EVERYONE'S FAITH MATTERS.

Jesus recognises real faith in him, whoever shows it. You can be an outsider, and looked down on. You can have no-one else to turn to, but you can always turn to Jesus. His care crosses social boundaries and religious barriers. He's no snob!

The woman was persistent when she turned to Jesus. She had faith that Jesus could drive out the demon. When Jesus saw that she didn't give up easily and gave him a good answer, he responded. Her answer was born of faith. She could not have given that answer unless she really believed in Jesus. She knew that she could trust in him.

The region of the Decapolis (the Ten Cities) is Gentile territory. The religious experts taught that these people weren't supposed to receive blessing from God. But Jesus responded to this woman's faith even though she came from this supposedly unclean area. Why? Because he could see that her faith was real because it was bold.

Pray boldly. Pray confidently. Don't insult God with little prayers as if he were only a little God. And stick at it.

READ THIS THEN PRAY:
"He cares for you." 1 Peter 5:7

Prayer: Thank you, Jesus, that you care for me. Help me not to speak to you as if you were mean and stingy. Amen.

FAITH IN JESUS. "Faith is being sure of what we hope for and certain of what we do not see." Hebrews 11:1. The Greek woman took her problems to Jesus. She had faith in him. Everyone else had failed her. He wouldn't.

Maps: Syria; Phoenicia. Pages 142–143.

DAY 17 MARK 8:1–21

During those days another large crowd gathered. Since they had nothing to eat, Jesus called his disciples to him and said, ² "I have compassion for these people; they have already been with me three days and have nothing to eat. ³ If I send them home hungry, they will collapse on the way, because some of them have come a long distance."

⁴ His disciples answered, "But where in this remote place can anyone get enough bread to feed them?"

⁵ "How many loaves do you have?" Jesus asked. "Seven," they replied.

⁶ He told the crowd to sit down on the ground. When he had taken the seven loaves and given thanks, he broke them and gave them to his disciples to set before the people, and they did so. ⁷ They had a few small fish as well; he gave thanks for them also and told the disciples to distribute them. ⁸ The people ate and were satisfied. Afterwards the disciples picked up seven basketfuls of broken pieces that were left over. ⁹ About four thousand men were present. And having sent them away, ¹⁰ he got into the boat with his disciples and went to the region of Dalmanutha.

¹¹ The Pharisees came and began to question Jesus. To test him, they asked him for a sign from heaven. ¹² He sighed deeply and said, "Why does this generation ask for a miraculous sign? I tell you the truth, no sign will be given to it." ¹³ Then he left them, got back into the boat and crossed to the other side.

¹⁴ The disciples had forgotten to bring bread, except for one loaf they had with them in the boat. ¹⁵ "Be careful," Jesus warned them. "Watch out for the yeast of the Pharisees and that of Herod."

¹⁶ They discussed this with one another and said, "It is because we have no bread."

¹⁷ Aware of their discussion, Jesus asked them: "Why are you talking about having no bread? Do you still not see or understand? Are your hearts hardened? ¹⁸ Do you have eyes but fail to see, and ears but fail to hear? And don't you remember? ¹⁹ When I broke the five loaves for the five thousand, how many basketfuls of pieces did you pick up?"

"Twelve," they replied.

20 "And when I broke the seven loaves for the four thousand, how many basketfuls of pieces did you pick up?" They answered, "Seven."

21 He said to them, "Do you still not understand?"

TURN OVER PAGE FOR THE DEVOTIONAL AND THINK SECTIONS.

DAY 17 MARK 8:1-21. AMAZING GRACE, AMAZING BLINDNESS.

Jesus repeats the earlier feeding miracle, but now he does it in Gentile territory. He's King of all – both Jew and Gentile. He gives his abundant grace to all – all peoples and nations and languages will be blessed through him. But the Pharisees, are waiting for him angrily when he comes ashore. They demand a sign to prove that he is God's King, the Christ. "No chance!" says Jesus. He does not have to prove himself to them, as if they were lords over him. They are blind because of the unbelief of their hearts. They cannot see what is staring them in the face: the promised Messiah is Jesus.

But Jesus fed 5,000 people, and then another 4,000 people. The disciples saw this and they still don't understand who Jesus is. They have the same disease as the Pharisees – the 'yeast' that Jesus warns against. This disease is that the disciples need Jesus but they don't realise it. They need him to feed their souls. Their hearts, like the hearts of the Pharisees, are hardened against him.

How terrible! Are you like the disciples? Are you unable to see how much you need Jesus? If you are we will see tomorrow how God sent a doctor for the spiritually blind.

 TRUE GRACE. God gives great gifts to all people. He lets rain fall on the fields of those people who believe in him and those who don't. He has given us a wonderful world to live in. It is sin that spoils this world - but every good and perfect gift comes from God. We have so much to thank him for. As well as this God gives us the gift of faith and eternal life without us having to do anything. This is what true grace is like. Think of what a wonderful blessing it is to be saved from your sin. Now think of what Jesus went through in order that we could receive this gift. We do not deserve it. Yet it is given to us freely.

UNBELIEF. This is a spiritual problem that will keep us out of heaven. If you do not believe in the Lord Jesus Christ you will not be saved from your sin. In the Book of Acts chapter 16 The Philippian Jailor asked Paul what he had to do to be saved from his sin. Paul told him to believe in the Lord Jesus Christ. Even when we believe in Jesus Christ we can sometimes struggle with unbelief. Jesus can help us with this - all we need to do is pray to him. Remember this when you come to Day 21.

READ THIS THEN PRAY:
"I will cleanse them from all the sin they have committed against me and will forgive all their sins of rebellion against me." Jeremiah 33:8

Prayer: Lord, help me to have a heart that believes that Jesus really is the King and Saviour. Forgive me when I can't understand what it means to follow him because my heart has been hardened by sin. Keep cleansing my heart. Amen.

Words: Gentile; Jews; Soul. Pages 126–130.
Who's Who: Messiah; Christ. Pages 130-132.
Boot Camp: Jesus' authority. Pages 135–141.

DAY 18 MARK 8:22–30

²² They came to Bethsaida, and some people brought a blind man and begged Jesus to touch him. ²³ He took the blind man by the hand and led him outside the village. When he had spat on the man's eyes and put his hands on him, Jesus asked, "Do you see anything?"

²⁴ He looked up and said, "I see people; they look like trees walking around."

²⁵ Once more Jesus put his hands on the man's eyes. Then his eyes were opened, his sight was restored, and he saw everything clearly. ²⁶ Jesus sent him home, saying, "Don't go into the village."

²⁷ Jesus and his disciples went on to the villages around Caesarea Philippi. On the way he asked them, "Who do people say I am?"

²⁸ They replied, "Some say John the Baptist; others say Elijah; and still others, one of the prophets."

²⁹ "But what about you?" he asked. "Who do you say I am?"

Peter answered, "You are the Christ."

³⁰ Jesus warned them not to tell anyone about him.

EARTHLY GLORY. Do you think more about the things you can buy today than about Jesus? Are you more concerned about what your friends think of you than about what God thinks of you? If you answer yes then you are more concerned about earthly glory than heavenly gain. When we think about Jesus and focus on God's word, when we long to please our Heavenly Father more than any other person, then we are storing up treasures in heaven. We are becoming more like Christ. Earthly things mean nothing in comparison to God's word and God's Son. Trust in Jesus to save you from your sins. Focus on what really matters: glorifying God.

Who's Who: Elijah; John the Baptist; Jesus Christ. Pages 131–134.
Maps: Caesarea Philippi. Pages 142–143.

DAY 18 MARK 8:22–30. TWO BLIND MEN SEE.

Two blind men are given sight. The first cannot see with his physical eyes until Jesus gives him sight. The second, Peter, cannot see spiritually until God the Father gives him sight.

The first healing is like a parable acted out with real human beings in order to help us make sense of what happens to Peter later on. The first blind man receives his sight bit by bit – first blurred, then clear. Peter will see spiritual truths gradually. The first blind man sees people, and he knows that they are people, but they look like trees walking. Peter will see a person, Jesus, and recognise him to be the Christ (he gets his identity right), but he won't see Jesus clearly until after the resurrection and the sending of the Spirit. The first man is warned not to tell anyone. So is Peter. Everyone will make the same mistake that Peter (and the rest of the disciples) were about to make and think of earthly glory, not heavenly gain. Only God can open the eyes of people so that they can clearly see who Jesus is and what he has done for them. We can tell others about Jesus. It is God who does the miracle and opens blind eyes.

READ THIS THEN PRAY:

"The god of this age has blinded the minds of unbelievers, so that they cannot see the light of the Gospel of the glory of Christ, who is the image of God. For we do not preach ourselves, but Jesus Christ as Lord, and ourselves as your servants for Jesus' sake. For God, who said, 'Let light shine out of darkness,' made his light shine in our hearts to give us the light of the knowledge of the glory of God in the face of Christ." 2 Corinthians 4:4-6

Prayer: Lord Jesus thank you that we can see clearly who you are and that our hearts can be changed to love you instead of loving sin. Give us the courage and the faith to tell others about you. Amen.

DAY 19 MARK 8:31–9:1

³¹ He then began to teach them that the Son of Man must suffer many things and be rejected by the elders, chief priests and teachers of the law, and that he must be killed and after three days rise again. ³² He spoke plainly about this, and Peter took him aside and began to rebuke him.

³³ But when Jesus turned and looked at his disciples, he rebuked Peter. "Get behind me, Satan!" he said. "You do not have in mind the things of God, but the things of men."

³⁴ Then he called the crowd to him along with his disciples and said: "If anyone would come after me, he must deny himself and take up his cross and follow me. ³⁵ For whoever wants to save his life will lose it, but whoever loses his life for me and for the Gospel will save it. ³⁶ What good is it for a man to gain the whole world, yet forfeit his soul? ³⁷ Or what can a man give in exchange for his soul? ³⁸ If anyone is ashamed of me and my words in this adulterous and sinful generation, the Son of Man will be ashamed of him when he comes in his Father's glory with the holy angels."

MARK 9:1

And he said to them, "I tell you the truth, some who are standing here will not taste death before they see the kingdom of God come with power."

YOUR SOUL. What is the price for your soul? It is so valuable there is no price that you could put on it. It is so precious that there is nothing that you could exchange for it. You have a soul that is more valuable than the world itself. In fact if you were to give your soul in exchange for all the riches and beauty of the whole world it would be a truly foolish act because you would gain nothing. The Bible says that the soul that sins shall die but your soul can be saved from sin by Jesus Christ. Eternal life for your soul is only obtained through believing in Jesus. Your soul and resurrected body will live forever with Christ if you believe in him. If you don't believe your soul and resurrected body will die forever in eternal punishment.

DAY 19 MARK 8:31–9:1. THE CROSS ON THE HORIZON.

Poor Peter! He didn't understand that Jesus came to save us and that the only way was for him to die on the cross. But then, you and I might not have understood that either.

We naturally want everything to go well in the way that the world thinks is good. The world thinks that success can't mean pain or loss. This is not the way that God looks at success. To be a 'successful' Christian is to be an obedient Christian. More than anything else, Jesus wanted to do his Father's will, even if that meant the cross. So if you and I want to follow him and be his disciples, we must want the same as Jesus – to do the Father's will not our own will. Or better, to make the Father's will our own. Even if it means suffering and loss. The way of Jesus is the way of the cross – every day! Every day you must want what God wants and follow him.

 READ THIS THEN PRAY:
"When you were dead in your sins and in the uncircumcision of your sinful nature, God made you alive with Christ. He forgave us all our sins." Colossians 2:13

Prayer: Lord Jesus, I know that the Father never let you down. After the cross came new life. Please help me to follow you – to be ready to die to self and sin, and to enjoy the new life that the Father gives. Help me not to be afraid to be a disciple. Amen.

Words: Adulterous. Pages 126–130.
Who's Who: Son of Man. Pages 131–134.

DAY 20 MARK 9:2-13

² After six days Jesus took Peter, James and John with him and led them up a high mountain, where they were all alone. There he was transfigured before them. ³ His clothes became dazzling white, whiter than anyone in the world could bleach them. ⁴ And there appeared before them Elijah and Moses, who were talking with Jesus.

⁵ Peter said to Jesus, "Rabbi, it is good for us to be here. Let us put up three shelters - one for you, one for Moses and one for Elijah." ⁶ (He did not know what to say, they were so frightened.)

⁷ Then a cloud appeared and enveloped them, and a voice came from the cloud: "This is my Son, whom I love. Listen to him!"

⁸ Suddenly, when they looked round, they no longer saw anyone with them except Jesus. ⁹ As they were coming down the mountain, Jesus gave them orders not to tell anyone what they had seen until the Son of Man had risen from the dead. ¹⁰ They kept the matter to themselves, discussing what "rising from the dead" meant. ¹¹ And they asked him, "Why do the teachers of the law say that Elijah must come first?"

¹² Jesus replied, "To be sure, Elijah does come first, and restores all things. Why then is it written that the Son of Man must suffer much and be rejected? ¹³ But I tell you, Elijah has come, and they have done to him everything they wished, just as it is written about him."

MESSIAH. The disciples talk about something that the teachers of the law had said. The teachers of the law taught that before the promised Messiah would come another Elijah would come. Jesus tells the disciples that this is true and that in fact has already happened. The second Elijah is John the Baptist. How did the people treat John the Baptist? What happened to him?

Words: Transfigured; Rabbi. Pages 126-130.
Who's who: Elijah; Moses; Malachi. Pages 131-134.

DAY 20 MARK 9:2–13. GOD'S GLORY ON THE MOUNTAIN.

The three men who go up the mountain with Jesus see Jesus in all his glory. They see God's King, God's great leader; they see a saviour; they see that suffering does not wipe out glory. They see Moses and Elijah as well – the two men whom the prophet Malachi connected with the last days (Malachi 4:4-6). It must have been a terrifying experience for them.

But they also see what they will share in heaven. Even though it will be hard to follow Jesus on earth, the glory of heaven awaits. God's glory is awesome. Whenever we read of people seeing it, they are struck down by it. But one day we won't be struck down by God's glory; one day we will see Jesus as he is and we will be made like him (1 John 3:2). One day his glory will be revealed not just to us but also in us (Romans 8:18)!

What an encouragement to keep going through the long hard trudge of this life, when you catch a glimpse of the wonderful place that you're going to! Don't give up – Jesus didn't.

 READ THIS THEN PRAY:
"Let us fix our eyes on Jesus, the author and perfecter of our faith, who for the joy set before him endured the cross, scorning its shame, and sat down at the right hand of the throne of God. Consider him who endured such opposition from sinful men, so that you will not grow weary and lose heart." Hebrews 12:2-3

Prayer: Thank you, Father, that Jesus kept going on the path that you laid out for him. He saw the glory that awaited him beyond the cross. Help me to walk with you through difficult times. Amen.

DAY 21 MARK 9:14—32

¹⁴ When they came to the other disciples, they saw a large crowd around them and the teachers of the law arguing with them. ¹⁵ As soon as all the people saw Jesus, they were overwhelmed with wonder and ran to greet him.

¹⁶ "What are you arguing with them about?" he asked.

¹⁷ A man in the crowd answered, "Teacher, I brought you my son, who is possessed by a spirit that has robbed him of speech. ¹⁸ Whenever it seizes him, it throws him to the ground. He foams at the mouth, gnashes his teeth and becomes rigid. I asked your disciples to drive out the spirit, but they could not."

¹⁹ "O unbelieving generation," Jesus replied, "how long shall I stay with you? How long shall I put up with you? Bring the boy to me."

²⁰ So they brought him. When the spirit saw Jesus, it immediately threw the boy into a convulsion. He fell to the ground and rolled around, foaming at the mouth.

²¹ Jesus asked the boy's father, "How long has he been like this?"

"From childhood," he answered. ²² "It has often thrown him into fire or water to kill him. But if you can do anything, take pity on us and help us."

²³ "'If you can'?" said Jesus. "Everything is possible for him who believes."

²⁴ Immediately the boy's father exclaimed, "I do believe; help me overcome my unbelief!"

²⁵ When Jesus saw that a crowd was running to the scene, he rebuked the evil spirit. "You deaf and mute spirit," he said, "I command you, come out of him and never enter him again."

²⁶ The spirit shrieked, convulsed him violently and came out. The boy looked so much like a corpse that many said, "He's dead." ²⁷ But Jesus took him by the hand and lifted him to his feet, and he stood up.

²⁸ After Jesus had gone indoors, his disciples asked him privately, "Why couldn't we drive it out?"

²⁹ He replied, "This kind can come out only by prayer."

[30] They left that place and passed through Galilee. Jesus did not want anyone to know where they were, [31] because he was teaching his disciples. He said to them, "The Son of Man is going to be betrayed into the hands of men. They will kill him, and after three days he will rise." [32] But they did not understand what he meant and were afraid to ask him about it.

TURN OVER PAGE FOR THE DEVOTIONAL AND THINK SECTIONS.

DAY 21 MARK 9:14–32. FOR NOW, IT'S EARTH.

No sooner are they down the mountain, than they are caught up in a human and spiritual storm. There's a disagreement between the teachers of the law and the disciples; a demon-possessed boy has not been cured. The disciples still don't understand what Jesus means about the coming cross. Things are messy. It can and will be the same for you. God works in the lives of those who believe in him – but his followers make mistakes.

Why are the disciples afraid to ask about the coming death of Jesus? Perhaps they are afraid of losing him. Perhaps they refuse to learn about the way in which the Messiah will save his people. Perhaps they are worried that what happens to Jesus will happen to them. What are you afraid of? Do you feel like backing down when being faithful to Jesus means facing opposition or pain? We all have that fear, but Jesus will only ever lead us to glory. It might mean following Jesus through pain and rejection. But it will lead to heaven. Jesus said "If anyone would come after me, he must deny himself and take up his cross daily and follow me," (Luke 9:23).

 CHRIST'S CHURCH. The church of Christ is growing in countries where it is illegal to own a Bible. Christians there can be put to death for their faith. However, the final destination of Christians is heaven. Getting there is a struggle but God never leaves us. He will give us strength.

READ THIS THEN PRAY:
"Neither death nor life, neither angels nor demons, neither the present nor the future, nor any powers, neither height nor depth, nor anything else in all creation, will be able to separate us from the love of God that is in Christ Jesus our Lord." Romans 8:37-39

Prayer: Lord, please give me courage to face up to the cost of following you. Thank you that Jesus showed his power over Satan here. Satan will not keep me from heaven if I am yours. Amen.

Who's Who: Demon; Disciples; Messiah. Pages 130-132.
Boot Camp: Jesus' authority; Crucifixion; Heaven. Pages 135–141.

DAY 22 MARK 9:33–50

They came to Capernaum. When he was in the house, he asked them, "What were you arguing about on the road?"

³⁴ But they kept quiet because on the way they had argued about who was the greatest.

³⁵ Sitting down, Jesus called the Twelve and said, "If anyone wants to be first, he must be the very last, and the servant of all."

³⁶ He took a little child and had him stand among them. Taking him in his arms, he said to them, ³⁷ "Whoever welcomes one of these little children in my name welcomes me; and whoever welcomes me does not welcome me but the one who sent me."

³⁸ "Teacher," said John, "we saw a man driving out demons in your name and we told him to stop, because he was not one of us."

³⁹ "Do not stop him," Jesus said. "No-one who does a miracle in my name can in the next moment say anything bad about me, ⁴⁰ for whoever is not against us is for us. ⁴¹ I tell you the truth, anyone who gives you a cup of water in my name because you belong to Christ will certainly not lose his reward.

⁴² "And if anyone causes one of these little ones who believe in me to sin, it would be better for him to be thrown into the sea with a large millstone tied around his neck. ⁴³ If your hand causes you to sin, cut it off. It is better for you to enter life maimed than with two hands to go into hell, where the fire never goes out. ⋯

⁴⁵ And if your foot causes you to sin, cut it off. It is better for you to enter life crippled than to have two feet and be thrown into hell. ⋯

⁴⁷ And if your eye causes you to sin, pluck it out. It is better for you to enter the kingdom of God with one eye than to have two eyes and be thrown into hell, ⁴⁸ where 'their worm does not die, and the fire is not quenched.'

⁴⁹ Everyone will be salted with fire. ⁵⁰ Salt is good, but if it loses its saltiness, how can you make it salty again? Have salt in yourselves, and be at peace with each other."

DAY 22 Mark 9:33–50. The Greatest and the Least.

Many arguments are caused by people wanting their own way instead of God's way. We want power and recognition. We want to be top of the heap. But those who follow Jesus should want to be different. They should be humble and trust God completely – like a little child. God's way is to put the other person first. The way up is the way down. We 'descend into greatness'.

We often want importance now – in this life. We forget that the next life will last longer. Better to spend this short life getting ready for the eternity that lies ahead. Better to say 'No' to sin now than to have to endure loss later. Do you want to be like Jesus? He endured the pain and humiliation of the cross for us and trusted his Father. He always looked ahead. Which life is the most important to you – this very short one or the next, everlasting life? If I could ask you in a thousand years from today, which life would you say was the one to concentrate on?

READ THIS THEN PRAY:
"Do not conform any longer to the pattern of this world, but be transformed by the renewing of your mind. Then you will be able to test and approve what God's will is—his good, pleasing and perfect will." Romans 12:2

Prayer: I need to put others first Lord. But the world teaches the opposite. Pease help me to get my values lined up with Jesus. If I need to say 'sorry' to someone, help me to do it today. Amen.

CHILDREN. Children in Jesus time were not considered important. But Jesus taught that children are important. People still look down on young people. If you are poor you can be ignored. If you are uneducated you can be dismissed. Jesus didn't treat people this way. Neither should we.

Words: Eternity. Pages 126–130.
Maps: Capernaum. Pages 142–143.

DAY 23 MARK 10:1–31

Jesus then left that place and went into the region of Judea and across the Jordan. Again crowds of people came to him, and as was his custom, he taught them.

² Some Pharisees came and tested him by asking, "Is it lawful for a man to divorce his wife?"

³ "What did Moses command you?" he replied.

⁴ They said, "Moses permitted a man to write a certificate of divorce and send her away."

⁵ "It was because your hearts were hard that Moses wrote you this law," Jesus replied. ⁶ "But at the beginning of creation God 'made them male and female'. ⁷ 'For this reason a man will leave his father and mother and be united to his wife, ⁸ and the two will become one flesh.' So they are no longer two, but one. ⁹ Therefore what God has joined together, let man not separate."

¹⁰ When they were in the house again, the disciples asked Jesus about this.

¹¹ He answered, "Anyone who divorces his wife and marries another woman commits adultery against her. ¹² And if she divorces her husband and marries another man, she commits adultery."

¹³ People were bringing little children to Jesus to have him touch them, but the disciples rebuked them. ¹⁴ When Jesus saw this, he was indignant. He said to them, "Let the little children come to me, and do not hinder them, for the kingdom of God belongs to such as these. ¹⁵ I tell you the truth, anyone who will not receive the kingdom of God like a little child will never enter it." ¹⁶ And he took the children in his arms, put his hands on them and blessed them.

¹⁷ As Jesus started on his way, a man ran up to him and fell on his knees before him. "Good teacher," he asked, "what must I do to inherit eternal life?"

¹⁸ "Why do you call me good?" Jesus answered. "No-one is good – except God alone. ¹⁹ You know the commandments: 'Do not murder, do not commit adultery, do not steal, do not give false testimony, do not defraud, honour your father and mother.'"

²⁰ "Teacher," he declared, "all these I have kept since I was a boy."

21 Jesus looked at him and loved him. "One thing you lack," he said. "Go, sell everything you have and give to the poor, and you will have treasure in heaven. Then come, follow me."

22 At this the man's face fell. He went away sad, because he had great wealth.

23 Jesus looked around and said to his disciples, "How hard it is for the rich to enter the kingdom of God!"

24 The disciples were amazed at his words. But Jesus said again, "Children, how hard it is to enter the kingdom of God! 25 It is easier for a camel to go through the eye of a needle than for a rich man to enter the kingdom of God."

26 The disciples were even more amazed, and said to each other, "Who then can be saved?"

27 Jesus looked at them and said, "With man this is impossible, but not with God; all things are possible with God."

28 Peter said to him, "We have left everything to follow you!"

29 "I tell you the truth," Jesus replied, "no-one who has left home or brothers or sisters or mother or father or children or fields for me and the Gospel 30 will fail to receive a hundred times as much in this present age (homes, brothers, sisters, mothers, children and fields – and with them, persecutions) and in the age to come, eternal life. 31 But many who are first will be last, and the last first."

TURN OVER PAGE FOR THE DEVOTIONAL AND THINK SECTIONS.

DAY 23 MARK 10:1–31. EXPECT THE UNEXPECTED!

Jesus is teaching again about living for the next life, and about child-like faith. He is reminding people how eternal life and faith are of more importance than those things that only last for a short while. But then there's the bit with the rich ruler. Why does Jesus tell him to do something that he knows is too hard? There are two reasons. First, Jesus is teaching that there are things that we can hold onto in this life that will stop us enjoying the next life. These things are obstacles to our salvation. We should let go of them. Second, Jesus wants the rich ruler to learn to be like a little child – weak, poor, but completely trusting. Jesus wants him to turn from his pride in his achievements and trust Jesus to get him to heaven. So Jesus takes him to the end of what he can do. The ruler could say 'Okay Lord, losing all my possessions is worth it for what I'll gain.' Or he could say 'I can't do that Lord, it's beyond me. So I'll trust you to get me to heaven.'

Instead he just walks away with his head down. He expected that he could get to heaven by his own works. But he can't. We, too, need to let go of this life and our own achievements and trust Jesus. Not easy, if we think that we can achieve a lot.

WHAT CAN YOU DO TO GET TO HEAVEN? Will going to church, reading the Bible and praying get you there? In fact, there is nothing you can do to win a place in heaven. Sin is too terrible and heaven is too wonderful for that. Even good people have sinned and sin deserves punishment. The good news is that Jesus loves sinners so much that he died for them. We all need to be forgiven and only Jesus can do that.

ETERNAL LIFE. This is a gift from God – no one earns it. It is only when you depend on Jesus to save you from your sins that you will get to heaven. Have you turned away from your sins and turned to Jesus? Have you accepted God's gift? Jesus is the way to heaven – the only way.

 READ THIS THEN PRAY:
"In the same way, any of you who does not give up everything he has cannot be my disciple." Luke 14:33

Prayer: Lord, if anything is coming between me and you please tell me what it is and help me to give it up. Amen.

Boot Camp: Getting started with you – Heaven. Pages 135–141.

DAY 24 MARK 10:32–45

³² They were on their way up to Jerusalem, with Jesus leading the way, and the disciples were astonished, while those who followed were afraid. Again he took the Twelve aside and told them what was going to happen to him. ³³ "We are going up to Jerusalem," he said, "and the Son of Man will be betrayed to the chief priests and teachers of the law. They will condemn him to death and will hand him over to the Gentiles, ³⁴ who will mock him and spit on him, flog him and kill him. Three days later he will rise."

³⁵ Then James and John, the sons of Zebedee, came to him. "Teacher," they said, "we want you to do for us whatever we ask."

³⁶ "What do you want me to do for you?" he asked.

³⁷ They replied, "Let one of us sit at your right and the other at your left in your glory."

³⁸ "You don't know what you are asking," Jesus said. "Can you drink the cup I drink or be baptised with the baptism I am baptised with?"

³⁹ "We can," they answered.

Jesus said to them, "You will drink the cup I drink and be baptised with the baptism I am baptised with, ⁴⁰ but to sit at my right or left is not for me to grant. These places belong to those for whom they have been prepared."

⁴¹ When the ten heard about this, they became indignant with James and John. ⁴² Jesus called them together and said, "You know that those who are regarded as rulers of the Gentiles lord it over them, and their high officials exercise authority over them. ⁴³ Not so with you. Instead, whoever wants to become great among you must be your servant, ⁴⁴ and whoever wants to be first must be slave of all. ⁴⁵ For even the Son of Man did not come to be served, but to serve, and to give his life as a ransom for many."

JESUS' DEATH. Why did Jesus die? Jesus knew what was ahead of him, but even then he was willing to go through with it – he was willing to die in order to save his people and to glorify God.

Maps: Jerusalem. Pages 142–143.

DAY 24 Mark 10:32–45. The Kingdom and the Cross.

How stupid can you get? When will these disciples understand that Jesus has to die in order to do what he's been sent to do? And why don't they understand that it's better for them if he does die on the cross? (See Boot Camp: Crucifixion. Page 138.) Why don't they see that if they want to have honour they have to reach it the way that Jesus did: through humiliation? How can they still not have grasped that Jesus came to serve and we, if we follow him, must learn to think and live like servants too?

Jesus is incredibly patient with people who keep thinking the way the world thinks and don't learn to think in the way of God's kingdom. He's a very loving teacher. It's just as well: when it comes to following Jesus, I can be just as slow to learn.

HUMILITY. Are you bossy? Do you ever boss or lord it over people who are younger or less able than you? That is not the way that Jesus behaves and it is not the way that his followers should behave. If you are a follower of Jesus Christ, if you love him, you will obey him. Jesus tells us that his followers are to be like servants. They are to be humble – they are to be more concerned about others than about themselves. They should think of others first and themselves last. A servant sees to the needs of others before they see to their own needs. Jesus was exactly like this.

READ THIS THEN PRAY:
"Because your love is better than life, my lips will glorify you." Psalm 63:3

Prayer: Thank you, Lord, that you kept going to the cross. Make me a servant too, for the sake of your glory. Amen.

DAY 25 MARK 10:46–11:11

46 Then they came to Jericho. As Jesus and his disciples, together with a large crowd, were leaving the city, a blind man, Bartimaeus (that is, the Son of Timaeus), was sitting by the roadside begging. 47 When he heard that it was Jesus of Nazareth, he began to shout, "Jesus, Son of David, have mercy on me!"

48 Many rebuked him and told him to be quiet, but he shouted all the more, "Son of David, have mercy on me!"

49 Jesus stopped and said, "Call him."

So they called to the blind man, "Cheer up! On your feet! He's calling you." 50 Throwing his cloak aside, he jumped to his feet and came to Jesus.

51 "What do you want me to do for you?" Jesus asked him.

The blind man said, "Rabbi, I want to see."

52 "Go," said Jesus, "your faith has healed you." Immediately he received his sight and followed Jesus along the road.

MARK 11:1–11

As they approached Jerusalem and came to Bethphage and Bethany at the Mount of Olives, Jesus sent two of his disciples, 2 saying to them, "Go to the village ahead of you, and just as you enter it, you will find a colt tied there, which no-one has ever ridden. Untie it and bring it here. 3 If anyone asks you, 'Why are you doing this?' tell him, 'The Lord needs it and will send it back here shortly.'"

4 They went and found a colt outside in the street, tied at a doorway. As they untied it, 5 some people standing there asked, "What are you doing, untying that colt?" 6 They answered as Jesus had told them to, and the people let them go. 7 When they brought the colt to Jesus and threw their cloaks over it, he sat on it. 8 Many people spread their cloaks on the road, while others spread branches they had cut in the fields. 9 Those who went ahead and those who followed shouted, "Hosanna!" "Blessed is he who comes in the name of the Lord!" 10 "Blessed is the coming kingdom of our father David!" "Hosanna in the highest!"

11 Jesus entered Jerusalem and went to the temple. He looked around at everything, but since it was already late, he went out to Bethany with the Twelve.

DAY 25 MARK 10:46–11:11. THE KING RIDES IN.

Mark does it again. He uses a healing miracle to show us something about Jesus. What did Bartimaeus shout out? What does he call Jesus? And what was David? Over which city was he King? And where is Jesus going to, as he passes through Jericho? What's the title of the one who needs the colt? What do the crowds shout about the one who rides in? So who is Jesus? He is 'the King who saves in the name of the Lord', coming to his city in fulfilment of a prophecy (Zechariah 9:9).

But does he ride up to a palace, enter a throne room, climb up onto a platform of honour and lift a gold crown onto his head? Not yet; not here. He goes to the temple, which should make people think of a heavenly throne and of sacrifice. He will go to Golgotha, the place of the skull. He will be raised up on a cross with a mocking notice about kingship over his head. He will be crowned with thorns. The King has come to establish his Kingdom through the cross and the grave. But from there he will go to the heavenly throne and rule the universe. Like the people then, we should be full of joy that Jesus is King. We should worship him. We should not turn away from him.

GOLGOTHA. Jesus was crucified just outside Jerusalem. It is also called the place of the skull. A place of death and disgrace where criminals were executed for their crimes. More information on Golgotha is on Page 83.

READ THIS THEN PRAY:
"Let us be thankful, and so worship God acceptably with reverence and awe." Hebrews 12:28

Prayer: Father, thank you for the Holy Spirit who inspired your servants to write the Bible and for teaching me to understand it. Amen.

Think Spot on God's Plan to Establish a Kingdom. Page 83.
Maps: Jericho; Jerusalem; Bethany; Mt. of Olives. Pages 142–143.

DAY 26 MARK 11:12–33

¹² The next day as they were leaving Bethany, Jesus was hungry. ¹³ Seeing in the distance a fig-tree in leaf, he went to find out if it had any fruit. When he reached it, he found nothing but leaves, because it was not the season for figs. ¹⁴ Then he said to the tree, "May no-one ever eat fruit from you again." And his disciples heard him say it.

¹⁵ On reaching Jerusalem, Jesus entered the temple area and began driving out those who were buying and selling there. He overturned the tables of the money-changers and the benches of those selling doves, ¹⁶ and would not allow anyone to carry merchandise through the temple courts. ¹⁷ And as he taught them, he said, "Is it not written: 'My house will be called a house of prayer for all nations'? But you have made it 'a den of robbers'."

¹⁸ The chief priests and the teachers of the law heard this and began looking for a way to kill him, for they feared him, because the whole crowd was amazed at his teaching.

¹⁹ When evening came, they went out of the city.

²⁰ In the morning, as they went along, they saw the fig-tree withered from the roots. ²¹ Peter remembered and said to Jesus, "Rabbi, look! The fig-tree you cursed has withered!"

²² "Have faith in God," Jesus answered. ²³ "I tell you the truth, if anyone says to this mountain, 'Go, throw yourself into the sea,' and does not doubt in his heart but believes that what he says will happen, it will be done for him. ²⁴ Therefore I tell you, whatever you ask for in prayer, believe that you have received it, and it will be yours. ²⁵ And when you stand praying, if you hold anything against anyone, forgive him, so that your Father in heaven may forgive you your sins." ⋯

²⁷ They arrived again in Jerusalem, and while Jesus was walking in the temple courts, the chief priests, the teachers of the law and the elders came to him. ²⁸ "By what authority are you doing these things?" they asked. "And who gave you authority to do this?"

²⁹ Jesus replied, "I will ask you one question. Answer me, and I will tell you by what authority I am doing these things. ³⁰ John's baptism – was it from heaven, or from men? Tell me!"

[31] They discussed it among themselves and said, "If we say, 'From heaven', he will ask, 'Then why didn't you believe him?' [32] But if we say, 'From men'...." (They feared the people, for everyone held that John really was a prophet.)

[33] So they answered Jesus, "We don't know." Jesus said, "Neither will I tell you by what authority I am doing these things."

TURN OVER PAGE FOR THE DEVOTIONAL AND THINK SECTIONS.

DAY 26 MARK 11:12–33. POOR TREE!

It seems a bit hard on the tree, doesn't it? But Jesus uses the tree as a picture of the people's hearts. This kind of fig bears its fruit just as the leaves are beginning to show. And 'season' means season for harvesting. The fig-tree should have figs on it that had not yet been harvested. Instead it only had leaves. At the time the kingly Son of God came to it, the tree should be bearing fruit. But it is barren just like the people. God's King has come to them. They should be full of the fruit of acceptance, repentance, worship and above all, joyful faith in him.

But they constantly argue with him. They hate him and reject him. They absolutely refuse to believe in him. The fig tree warns them that if they keep on like that, they will be as cursed as the fig-tree is. They will wither and die as a people.

One more thing. Notice the power of Jesus' word. He says that our speech can have power from God also. That power comes from what? From faith in God. What you say today can affect people for eternity.

 READ THIS THEN PRAY:
"But the fruit of the Spirit is love, joy, peace, patience, kindness, goodness, faithfulness, gentleness and self-control. Against such things there is no law." Galatians 5: 22-23

Prayer: Lord, you have every right to expect my life to be fruitful. You have appointed me to bear the Spirit's fruit. You have said that if I abide in you and your word remains in me, I shall bear fruit. Please help me to keep trusting you, Almighty King. Amen.

FAITH. What is it about faith? It is amazing what faith in God achieves. It is not because our faith is amazing that it accomplishes anything – it is because of the God that we have our faith in.

 GOLGOTHA. This is also known as The place of the skull. It is situated just outside Jerusalem. It wasn't a green and pleasant place. It wasn't somewhere peaceful and quiet. It was truly terrible. A place of execution. The cross was a method of capital punishment. Jesus went through more suffering than we can ever imagine. He did this in order to save sinners from the punishment of eternal death. Instead of death he gives the gift of eternal life to those who trust in him.

 GOD'S PLAN. What is God's plan? God's plan is to establish his Kingdom. God's plan from before the beginning of the world was that sinners would be saved. By ourselves we cannot become part of God's kingdom. Sin stops us. But Jesus Christ's death on the cross has covered the sin of those who have believed in him. They are brought into God's kingdom. God's kingdom grows and is established because of Jesus' death on the cross and his resurrection from the dead.

Words: Eternity. Pages 126–130.
Who's Who: Chief Priests; John the Baptist. Pages 131–134.
Maps: Bethany; Jerusalem. Pages 142–143.

DAY 27 MARK 11:12-33

[12] The next day as they were leaving Bethany, Jesus was hungry. [13] Seeing in the distance a fig-tree in leaf, he went to find out if it had any fruit. When he reached it, he found nothing but leaves, because it was not the season for figs. [14] Then he said to the tree, "May no-one ever eat fruit from you again." And his disciples heard him say it.

[15] On reaching Jerusalem, Jesus entered the temple area and began driving out those who were buying and selling there. He overturned the tables of the money-changers and the benches of those selling doves, [16] and would not allow anyone to carry merchandise through the temple courts. [17] And as he taught them, he said, "Is it not written: 'My house will be called a house of prayer for all nations'?

But you have made it 'a den of robbers'."

[18] The chief priests and the teachers of the law heard this and began looking for a way to kill him, for they feared him, because the whole crowd was amazed at his teaching.

[19] When evening came, they went out of the city.

[20] In the morning, as they went along, they saw the fig-tree withered from the roots. [21] Peter remembered and said to Jesus, "Rabbi, look! The fig-tree you cursed has withered!"

[22] "Have faith in God," Jesus answered. [23] "I tell you the truth, if anyone says to this mountain, 'Go, throw yourself into the sea,' and does not doubt in his heart but believes that what he says will happen, it will be done for him. [24] Therefore I tell you, whatever you ask for in prayer, believe that you have received it, and it will be yours. [25] And when you stand praying, if you hold anything against anyone, forgive him, so that your Father in heaven may forgive you your sins." ...

[27] They arrived again in Jerusalem, and while Jesus was walking in the temple courts, the chief priests, the teachers of the law and the elders came to him. [28] "By what authority are you doing these things?" they asked. "And who gave you authority to do this?"

[29] Jesus replied, "I will ask you one question. Answer me, and I will tell you by what authority I am doing these things. [30] John's baptism – was it from heaven, or from men? Tell me!"

[31] They discussed it among themselves and said, "If we say, 'From

heaven', he will ask, 'Then why didn't you believe him?' [32] But if we say, 'From men'...." (They feared the people, for everyone held that John really was a prophet.)

[33] So they answered Jesus, "We don't know."

Jesus said, "Neither will I tell you by what authority I am doing these things."

TURN OVER PAGE FOR THE DEVOTIONAL AND THINK SECTIONS.

DAY 27 MARK 11:12–33. PURIFYING THE TEMPLE.

It's verses 15 to 19 that we will be thinking about today. The Old Testament said that the Lord would suddenly come to his temple and that he would be like a refiner's fire, purging all the evil dross out of it.

Why does Jesus do this? Well, look carefully at where he does it. The money-changers and the sacrifice-sellers are not in the temple, but in what Mark calls 'the temple area'. That is, the court of the Gentiles. That's why Jesus talks about it being a place of prayer 'for all nations'. Jesus is restoring the blessing of access to God's presence in the temple to Gentiles. He's clearing the way for all nations to come into his Kingdom.

But the people who thought that they owned the temple were furious and began to plot his death. Their little empire was being overturned by God's true King.

I'm so glad that Jesus cleaned out the court of the Gentiles. I am a Gentile. And I'm so glad that he was prepared to endure scorn and hatred to do that. Truly he is the King of all peoples and the King of love.

HOW CAN I FIND GOD? Jesus wanted all people to have access to God – Jews and Gentiles. We can now have access to God because Jesus Christ has gained this access for us by dying on the cross. You just have to come to God in the name of his Son, Jesus Christ.

WHERE IS GOD? God is everywhere at all times. You can worship God and speak with him at any time and in any place.

WHERE CAN I WORSHIP GOD? In the Bible people often went to the temple or synagogue to worship God. They sometimes called this The House of God. Jesus threw the moneylenders out of the temple as he had great respect for God's house. Today you can worship God anywhere - but there are specific places where Christ's followers meet to worship him. These are sometimes called churches. However the word church should really be used to describe the group of people who love and worship Jesus. Across the world the church of Christ meets together to praise God's name. They meet in buildings, community halls or homes. They meet by rivers, in fields, or under trees. They can meet anywhere - because wherever they are God is with them. Do you long to worship the Lord Jesus? Going to church to worship God is a good way to honour God and to grow as a Christian.

 READ THIS THEN PRAY:
"At that time they will call Jerusalem The Throne of the LORD, and all nations will gather in Jerusalem to honour the name of the LORD. No longer will they follow the stubbornness of their evil hearts." Jeremiah 3:17

Prayer: Lord, thank you that your mission is to bring people into your Kingdom from every nation, language tribe and tongue. Thank you that your mission is being fulfilled now through your disciples. Help me to work with you to bring more people to worship King Jesus and to experience your love and grace. Amen.

Words: Synagogue; Temple; Worship; Rabbi. Pages 126–130.
Who's Who: Chief Priests; John the Baptist; Jeremiah. Pages 131–134.
Maps: Bethany; Jerusalem. Pages 142–143.

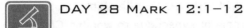

DAY 28 MARK 12:1–12

He then began to speak to them in parables: "A man planted a vineyard. He put a wall around it, dug a pit for the winepress and built a watchtower. Then he rented the vineyard to some farmers and went away on a journey. ² At harvest time he sent a servant to the tenants to collect from them some of the fruit of the vineyard. ³ But they seized him, beat him and sent him away empty-handed. ⁴ Then he sent another servant to them; they struck this man on the head and treated him shamefully. ⁵ He sent still another, and that one they killed. He sent many others; some of them they beat, others they killed.

⁶ He had one left to send, a son, whom he loved. He sent him last of all, saying, 'They will respect my son.'

⁷ But the tenants said to one another, 'This is the heir. Come, let's kill him, and the inheritance will be ours.' ⁸ So they took him and killed him, and threw him out of the vineyard. ⁹ "What then will the owner of the vineyard do? He will come and kill those tenants and give the vineyard to others. ¹⁰ Haven't you read this scripture: 'The stone the builders rejected has become the capstone; ¹¹ the Lord has done this, and it is marvellous in our eyes'?" ¹² Then they looked for a way to arrest him because they knew he had spoken the parable against them. But they were afraid of the crowd; so they left him and went away.

JUDGE. Jesus used images that people could understand. The Pharisees understood and they still did not repent. This is a warning to us. When we read God's word we must obey it. If we disobey we are rejecting Jesus Christ just as the Pharisees did. Jesus will one day be our Judge if we turn away from him. Right now he can be your Saviour. Repent of your sins and turn to him.

DAY 28 MARK 12:1–12. WICKEDNESS CRUSHED.

Jesus makes a very sharp-pointed, public statement against the religious rulers. The vineyard is an Old Testament picture of Israel and the temple. The tenants are the religious rulers and the people who follow them. The servants are the prophets whom God has sent again and again, looking for the fruit of repentance and faith. They have been constantly abused and rejected and killed.

The son is Jesus whom they must surely respect and submit to. But do they? As Jesus has kept telling the disciples, he will die at the hands of sinful men.

But these men will be judged. Jesus uses the image of stones and buildings. (He is in the temple area, remember, which was still a bit of a building site.) Jesus uses the image of a huge, heavy capstone from a column or arch. Now the capstone was sometimes used as a means of execution. It was raised with ropes on a frame and a condemned man was stretched out beneath it. Then it was dropped on his head. Jesus said when describing the capstone that it had been rejected before it was chosen for this elevated position. Jesus was also rejected by wicked men. The Pharisees realised what this story really meant. They had just been told that God would judge them through Jesus.

READ THIS THEN PRAY:
"Whoever believes in Christ is not condemned, but whoever does not believe stands condemned already." John 3:18

Prayer: Lord, you are the just judge of all. Those who reject you Lord Jesus, will be condemned for doing so. Help me not to keep the Gospel from those who are rejecting you now. Amen.

DAY 29 MARK 12:13–40

13 Later they sent some of the Pharisees and Herodians to Jesus to catch him in his words. 14 They came to him and said, "Teacher, we know you are a man of integrity. You aren't swayed by men, because you pay no attention to who they are; but you teach the way of God in accordance with the truth. Is it right to pay taxes to Caesar or not? 15 Should we pay or shouldn't we?"

But Jesus knew their hypocrisy. "Why are you trying to trap me?" he asked. "Bring me a denarius and let me look at it." 16 They brought the coin, and he asked them, "Whose portrait is this? And whose inscription?"

"Caesar's," they replied.

17 Then Jesus said to them, "Give to Caesar what is Caesar's and to God what is God's."

And they were amazed at him.

18 Then the Sadducees, who say there is no resurrection, came to him with a question. 19 "Teacher," they said, "Moses wrote for us that if a man's brother dies and leaves a wife but no children, the man must marry the widow and have children for his brother. 20 Now there were seven brothers. The first one married and died without leaving any children. 21 The second one married the widow, but he also died, leaving no child. It was the same with the third. 22 In fact, none of the seven left any children. Last of all, the woman died too. 23 At the resurrection whose wife will she be, since the seven were married to her?"

24 Jesus replied, "Are you not in error because you do not know the Scriptures or the power of God? 25 When the dead rise, they will neither marry nor be given in marriage; they will be like the angels in heaven. 26 Now about the dead rising – have you not read in the book of Moses, in the account of the bush, how God said to him, 'I am the God of Abraham, the God of Isaac, and the God of Jacob'? 27 He is not the God of the dead, but of the living. You are badly mistaken!"

28 One of the teachers of the law came and heard them debating. Noticing that Jesus had given them a good answer, he asked him, "Of all the commandments, which is the most important?"

²⁹ "The most important one," answered Jesus, "is this: 'Hear, O Israel, the Lord our God, the Lord is one. ³⁰ Love the Lord your God with all your heart and with all your soul and with all your mind and with all your strength.' ³¹ The second is this: 'Love your neighbour as yourself.' There is no commandment greater than these."

³² "Well said, teacher," the man replied. "You are right in saying that God is one and there is no other but him. ³³ To love him with all your heart, with all your understanding and with all your strength, and to love your neighbour as yourself is more important than all burnt offerings and sacrifices."

³⁴ When Jesus saw that he had answered wisely, he said to him, "You are not far from the kingdom of God." And from then on no-one dared ask him any more questions.

³⁵ While Jesus was teaching in the temple courts, he asked, "How is it that the teachers of the law say that the Christ is the Son of David? ³⁶ David himself, speaking by the Holy Spirit, declared:

"'The Lord said to my Lord: "Sit at my right hand until I put your enemies under your feet."'

³⁷ David himself calls him 'Lord'. How then can he be his son?"

The large crowd listened to him with delight.

³⁸ As he taught, Jesus said, "Watch out for the teachers of the law. They like to walk around in flowing robes and be greeted in the market-places, ³⁹ and have the most important seats in the synagogues and the places of honour at banquets. ⁴⁰ They devour widows' houses and for a show make lengthy prayers. Such men will be punished most severely."

TURN OVER PAGE FOR THE DEVOTIONAL AND THINK SECTIONS.

DAY 29 MARK 12:13–40. BAD QUESTIONS, GOOD ANSWERS.

Three tricky questions, all designed to make Jesus say something that they could arrest him for and have him killed.
Jesus amazes everyone with his brilliant answers. He's the cleverest teacher in the world and his enemies haven't a chance!
But notice that one of them – the teacher of the law, is not so bad. He sees why Jesus' answer is good. Jesus sums up everything that, according to the Ten Commandments, God looked for from his people.

It's all about love. What God looks for from us is what he is full of himself. We are made to reflect his character: to bear his image, just as a Roman coin bore Caesar's image. So we fulfil all God's commandments as we give to God that which bears his image – ourselves. He has every right to expect us to show what he is like: to live and love his way.

 HOW DO WE KNOW THE TRUTH? God's word is a good tool for us to use in our daily life. It shows us how to live and how not to live. And by reading God's word we can tell if others are truly following him or not. In fact everything about God's word is true – it is the one book that we know we can rely on. God wrote it after all!

Words: Denarius. Pages 126–130.
Who's Who: Jesus Son of David; Pharisees; Herodians; Caesar; Sadducees; Moses; Abraham; Isaac; Jacob; Holy Spirit; David. Pages 131–134.
Boot Camp: The Ten Commandments. Pages 135–141.

WHAT DID JESUS DO? Jesus got the better of his opponents. They tried to trick him, but his questions totally stumped them! Jesus also warns us to watch out for those people who say they follow God but in actual fact behave in a way that is against God's law.

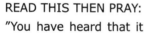 READ THIS THEN PRAY:
"You have heard that it was said, 'Love your neighbour and hate your enemy.' But I tell you: Love your enemies and pray for those who persecute you, that you may be sons of your Father in heaven. He causes his sun to rise on the evil and the good, and sends rain on the righteous and the unrighteous." Matthew 5:43-45

Prayer: Lord, help me to love like you do. Help me to love my enemies; to love sinners like me; to love without conditions; to love generously. Help me to live your way as an offering to you today. Amen.

DAY 30 MARK 12:41-44

⁴¹ Jesus sat down opposite the place where the offerings were put and watched the crowd putting their money into the temple treasury. Many rich people threw in large amounts. ⁴² But a poor widow came and put in two very small copper coins, worth only a fraction of a penny.

⁴³ Calling his disciples to him, Jesus said, "I tell you the truth, this poor widow has put more into the treasury than all the others. ⁴⁴ They all gave out of their wealth; but she, out of her poverty, put in everything – all she had to live on."

GOD'S WORK. How can I work for God? You may not have a lot of money now but there may be a time in the future when God blesses you with a job, a car, even a house.

Be sure to use God's gift for his glory. Be hospitable and welcome people to your home. Be willing to use your car to help others who are working for God's kingdom. Do not hold onto your money selfishly as if it was all yours. Instead be like the early Christians who were willing to sell those things that they didn't need in order to give money to God's work and to other needy Christians. (Acts 4:32–35.)

DAY 30 MARK 12:41–44. A POOR WIDOW AND A KIND KING.

You don't need to give God a lot of money. It's your heart that he's interested in. Rich people can give piles of money to the church but they can use their giving to show off and boost their egos.

That went on at the temple in Jerusalem. After teaching, Jesus sat and watched people putting their offerings in the boxes. Many were making a big fuss about it. 'Look at me,' they were saying.

But then a poor widow came along. She would have had no regular income and nothing to sell to get money. She put in a tiny amount of money – nothing, compared to the rich show-offs. Yet Jesus thought that she was an example of how to give to God.

Why? Because she gave everything that she had. And it was all that she had to live on. She gave away what she needed for buying her next bit of food. She thought that God was worth everything, and she trusted God to provide for her.

The wealthy often despised poor widows, but Jesus was full of kindness; he noticed what the crowd ignored. He respected the one that the crowd detested. He will notice when you only put in a little because that's all you've got. He will not despise you. He is kind. You can trust him to provide for you.

 READ THIS THEN PRAY:
"'For I know the plans I have for you,' declares the LORD, 'plans to prosper you and not to harm you, plans to give you hope and a future.'" Jeremiah 29:11

Prayer: I can be so mean and insecure when it comes to money, Lord. You know that I don't have much. But you can have all that I have. I trust you with my future and will not give in to fear. Thank you that Jesus is my kind friend. Amen.

Boot Camp: Getting started with God. Pages 135–141.

DAY 31 MARK 13:1-37

As he was leaving the temple, one of his disciples said to him, "Look, Teacher! What massive stones! What magnificent buildings!"

2 "Do you see all these great buildings?" replied Jesus. "Not one stone here will be left on another; every one will be thrown down."

3 As Jesus was sitting on the Mount of Olives opposite the temple, Peter, James, John and Andrew asked him privately, 4 "Tell us, when will these things happen? And what will be the sign that they are all about to be fulfilled?"

5 Jesus said to them: "Watch out that no-one deceives you. 6 Many will come in my name, claiming, 'I am he,' and will deceive many. 7 When you hear of wars and rumours of wars, do not be alarmed. Such things must happen, but the end is still to come. 8 Nation will rise against nation, and kingdom against kingdom. There will be earthquakes in various places, and famines. These are the beginning of birth-pains.

9 "You must be on your guard. You will be handed over to the local councils and flogged in the synagogues. On account of me you will stand before governors and kings as witnesses to them. 10 And the Gospel must first be preached to all nations. 11 Whenever you are arrested and brought to trial, do not worry beforehand about what to say. Just say whatever is given you at the time, for it is not you speaking, but the Holy Spirit.

12 "Brother will betray brother to death, and a father his child. Children will rebel against their parents and have them put to death. 13 All men will hate you because of me, but he who stands firm to the end will be saved.

14 "When you see 'the abomination that causes desolation' standing where it does not belong - let the reader understand – then let those who are in Judea flee to the mountains. 15 Let no-one on the roof of his house go down or enter the house to take anything out. 16 Let no-one in the field go back to get his cloak. 17 How dreadful it will be in those days for pregnant women and nursing mothers! 18 Pray that this will not take place in winter, 19 because those will be days of distress unequalled from the beginning, when God created

the world, until now – and never to be equalled again. ²⁰ If the Lord had not cut short those days, no-one would survive. But for the sake of the elect, whom he has chosen, he has shortened them. ²¹ At that time if anyone says to you, 'Look, here is the Christ!' or, 'Look, there he is!' Do not believe it. ²² For false Christs and false prophets will appear and perform signs and miracles to deceive the elect – if that were possible. ²³ So be on your guard; I have told you everything ahead of time.

²⁴ "But in those days, following that distress, the sun will be darkened, and the moon will not give its light; ²⁵ the stars will fall from the sky, and the heavenly bodies will be shaken. ²⁶ At that time men will see the Son of Man coming in clouds with great power and glory. ²⁷ And he will send his angels and gather his elect from the four winds, from the ends of the earth to the ends of the heavens.

²⁸ "Now learn this lesson from the fig-tree: As soon as its twigs get tender and its leaves come out, you know that summer is near. ²⁹ Even so, when you see these things happening, you know that it is near, right at the door. ³⁰ I tell you the truth, this generation will certainly not pass away until all these things have happened. ³¹ Heaven and earth will pass away, but my words will never pass away.

³² "No-one knows about that day or hour, not even the angels in heaven, nor the Son, but only the Father. ³³ Be on guard! Be alert! You do not know when that time will come. ³⁴ It's like a man going away: He leaves his house and puts his servants in charge, each with his assigned task, and tells the one at the door to keep watch.

³⁵ "Therefore keep watch because you do not know when the owner of the house will come back – whether in the evening, or at midnight, or when the cock crows, or at dawn. ³⁶ If he comes suddenly, do not let him find you sleeping. ³⁷ What I say to you, I say to everyone: 'Watch!'"

TURN OVER PAGE FOR THE DEVOTIONAL AND THINK SECTIONS.

DAY 31 MARK 13:1–37. WATCH OUT! THE KING'S COMING BACK.

It's impossible to split up this chapter because it's all on the same theme: the return of Jesus. It goes like this. The disciples think that the temple building is rock-solid, but Jesus says:

A day of total destruction will come. It will get worse for the church before it gets better. There will be many wars and nature will be in turmoil, too. Christians will be persecuted, but the Spirit will give the right words for us to be able to testify to Jesus. The Gospel will reach all the people-groups of the earth. When things get really dreadful for the church, then we will know that the King will soon return from heaven. So watch out. Be ready. Don't be caught out. He could come back at any minute: no-one, not even Jesus, knows the day or the time. Live as if it will be tonight.

Do you believe it? You'd better!

PERSECUTION? Jesus has told us that because he was hated by people in the world who did not believe in him those people who followed him would also be hated.

So persecution is something that we should expect. Persecution is being unfairly and cruelly treated because of what we believe and is something that we can expect if we follow Jesus. People will try and make things difficult for Christians. Jesus said in Matthew chapter 5 that those who are persecuted are blessed, or happy, for the Kingdom of Heaven belongs to them. Jesus has told us that when we are treated wrongly and have to suffer for loving Jesus we can rejoice because there will be a great reward for us in heaven.

HOW DO I TELL OTHERS ABOUT JESUS? Perhaps you don't know what to say to people who don't believe in Jesus Christ. You may even be criticised, bullied or worse because of your faith in God. Remember what Jesus said: Whenever you are arrested and brought to trial, do not worry beforehand about what to say. Just say whatever is given you at the time, for it is not you speaking, but the Holy Spirit. There will be times when you have to stand up and tell people what you believe, whether they want to hear you or not. Don't be afraid to say what is on your heart. If you love the Lord the Holy Spirit is with you and will give you the right words to say.

READ THIS THEN PRAY:
"But be sure to fear the LORD and serve him faithfully with all your heart; consider what great things he has done for you." 1 Samuel 12:24

Prayer: Lord, I know that you will return and bring in your Kingdom. Help me to be brave, faithful and ready. Amen.

DAY 32 MARK 14:1–11

Now the Passover and the Feast of Unleavened Bread were only two days away, and the chief priests and the teachers of the law were looking for some sly way to arrest Jesus and kill him. ² "But not during the Feast," they said, "or the people may riot."

³ While he was in Bethany, reclining at the table in the home of a man known as Simon the Leper, a woman came with an alabaster jar of very expensive perfume, made of pure nard. She broke the jar and poured the perfume on his head. ⁴ Some of those present were saying indignantly to one another, "Why this waste of perfume? ⁵ It could have been sold for more than a year's wages and the money given to the poor." And they rebuked her harshly.

⁶ "Leave her alone," said Jesus. "Why are you bothering her? She has done a beautiful thing to me. ⁷ The poor you will always have with you, and you can help them any time you want. But you will not always have me. ⁸ She did what she could. She poured perfume on my body beforehand to prepare for my burial. ⁹ I tell you the truth, wherever the Gospel is preached throughout the world, what she has done will also be told, in memory of her."

¹⁰ Then Judas Iscariot, one of the Twelve, went to the chief priests to betray Jesus to them. ¹¹ They were delighted to hear this and promised to give him money. So he watched for an opportunity to hand him over.

UNDERSTANDING. The woman understood what the disciples failed to understand. Jesus said, "She poured perfume on my body beforehand to prepare for my burial."

She knew that Jesus had come to die – only God could have shown her that. It is only God's Spirit that can reveal to you that you are a sinner, and need to be saved. Ask him to show you your need of Jesus Christ and salvation.

Words: Passover; Alabaster; Pure nard. Pages 126–130.
Boot Camp: Old Testament, Exodus and the Passover. Pages 135–141.

DAY 32 MARK 14:1–11. A BEAUTIFUL THING.

The religious leaders are full of hatred and cunning and cowardice. But in the midst of all this, a beautiful thing happens. The jar of ointment is incredibly expensive. It would probably have been her bride-price: entirely hers and too expensive for her ever to replace. She enters a room full of men, some of whom looked at her with disgust. They are horrible, vile men who have no love for the Saviour and an entirely wrong set of values. What they say is perhaps technically true but their hearts are far from right. She, on the other hand, is full of love for the Saviour. She understands that he is about to die, and has the values of the Kingdom. Whatever we do that lovingly honours King Jesus is right. So as the fragrance of her love fills the room, Jesus springs to her defence and honours her.

Do you think that she counted it as loss to pour out all that ointment? Did she go home regretting what she'd done? I think not. I think she went home glad and blessed. But that's how love works. To give what is most precious is no loss, but gain. The more precious our gift, the better.

Judas can't stand such beauty and such lavish expenditure. He decides at that moment that he's against Jesus and his Kingdom. He knows that the leaders will listen to him now. He'll grab the cash and run.

 READ THIS THEN PRAY:
"Each man should give what he has decided in his heart to give, not reluctantly or under compulsion, for God loves a cheerful giver." 2 Corinthians 9:7

Prayer: Lord Jesus, may my love never grow cold. Give me greater joy through giving to Jesus than I can ever get through hoarding money. Amen.

DAY 33 MARK 14:12–31

¹² On the first day of the Feast of Unleavened Bread, when it was customary to sacrifice the Passover lamb, Jesus' disciples asked him, "Where do you want us to go and make preparations for you to eat the Passover?"

¹³ So he sent two of his disciples, telling them, "Go into the city, and a man carrying a jar of water will meet you. Follow him. ¹⁴ Say to the owner of the house he enters, 'The Teacher asks: Where is my guest room, where I may eat the Passover with my disciples?' ¹⁵ He will show you a large upper room, furnished and ready. Make preparations for us there."

¹⁶ The disciples left, went into the city and found things just as Jesus had told them. So they prepared the Passover.

¹⁷ When evening came, Jesus arrived with the Twelve. ¹⁸ While they were reclining at the table eating, he said, "I tell you the truth, one of you will betray me – one who is eating with me."

¹⁹ They were saddened, and one by one they said to him, "Surely not I?"

²⁰ "It is one of the Twelve," he replied, "one who dips bread into the bowl with me. ²¹ The Son of Man will go just as it is written about him. But woe to that man who betrays the Son of Man! It would be better for him if he had not been born."

²² While they were eating, Jesus took bread, gave thanks and broke it, and gave it to his disciples, saying, "Take it; this is my body."

²³ Then he took the cup, gave thanks and offered it to them, and they all drank from it.

²⁴ "This is my blood of the covenant, which is poured out for many," he said to them. ²⁵ "I tell you the truth, I will not drink again of the fruit of the vine until that day when I drink it anew in the kingdom of God."

²⁶ When they had sung a hymn, they went out to the Mount of Olives.

²⁷ "You will all fall away," Jesus told them, "for it is written: "'I will strike the shepherd, and the sheep will be scattered.'

[28] But after I have risen, I will go ahead of you into Galilee."

[29] Peter declared, "Even if all fall away, I will not." [30] "I tell you the truth," Jesus answered, "today – yes, tonight – before the cock crows twice you yourself will disown me three times."

[31] But Peter insisted emphatically, "Even if I have to die with you, I will never disown you." And all the others said the same.

TURN OVER PAGE FOR THE DEVOTIONAL AND THINK SECTIONS.

DAY 33 MARK 14:12–31. OUR PASSOVER LAMB.

Jesus' death draws near. His betrayer is set on his plan. Sacrificial death, blood protecting from judgement, exodus and escape from captivity for God's people – all these things are in the air at Passover time. During the Passover meal, Jesus takes all the imagery of food and drink, and all the hopes of the coming Kingdom, and says that they all speak of him.

When we take the bread and wine and remember the death of Jesus, we remember that it is by his death on the cross – the breaking of his body and the shedding of his blood – that we are freed from the power of death. He died in our place. We also remember that another feast lies ahead: the great feast in heaven when the Kingdom of God is revealed in all its fullness and all God's people are gathered together. We don't want to fail Jesus but even if we do deny him – like Peter was soon to do – we will all be gathered together in heaven because of his death for us; so great is the power of the cross.

THE CROSS. How can a cross be powerful? This cross is powerful because of the one who died on it. Christ has the real power – not the wood and the nails. Jesus was obedient to his Father and willing to die in the place of his people. It is through him we can have eternal life.

IS JESUS A WEAK KING?: Jesus is the King of kings because he is God's chosen and promised Saviour for the whole world. But surely a strong King would not be mocked and whipped and killed? Is this then a sign of weakness? No! It's quite the opposite. Jesus was willing to suffer and die in order to save his people from their sins. It is his strength that brought him to death, not weakness. The King of kings was fully in control even up to the moment of his death. Nobody took his life away, he willingly gave it for sinners. See also Words: King of the Jews. Pages 126–130.

SACRIFICIAL DEATH: Throughout Jewish history lambs without flaws or defects were chosen as sacrifices to make amends for sin. But these sacrifices had to be repeated, year in, year out. They were just a foreshadowing or a picture of the great sacrifice which was to come - the sacrifice of the spotless Lamb of God - Jesus Christ. His was the ultimate sacrifice. No other is now required. He has atoned for the sin of his people. He has covered the sin of his people. So for those who believe in the Lord Jesus Christ sin has been blotted out. The obstacle of guilt that comes between them and God has been removed.

READ THIS THEN PRAY:
"The LORD lives! Praise be to my Rock! Exalted be God, the Rock, my Saviour!" 2 Samuel 22:47

Prayer: How can we praise you, our heavenly friend, for all that you have done for us? Our love sometimes fails, but your work never fails. Help us never to forget the cross. Amen.

Words: Passover; Passover lamb. Pages 126–130.
Boot Camp: Passover; Exodus. Pages 135–141.

DAY 34 MARK 14:32-42

³² They went to a place called Gethsemane, and Jesus said to his disciples, "Sit here while I pray." ³³ He took Peter, James and John along with him, and he began to be deeply distressed and troubled. ³⁴ "My soul is overwhelmed with sorrow to the point of death," he said to them. "Stay here and keep watch."

³⁵ Going a little farther, he fell to the ground and prayed that if possible the hour might pass from him. ³⁶ "Abba, Father," he said, "everything is possible for you. Take this cup from me. Yet not what I will, but what you will."

³⁷ Then he returned to his disciples and found them sleeping. "Simon," he said to Peter, "are you asleep? Could you not keep watch for one hour? ³⁸ Watch and pray so that you will not fall into temptation. The spirit is willing, but the body is weak."

³⁹ Once more he went away and prayed the same thing. ⁴⁰ When he came back, he again found them sleeping, because their eyes were heavy. They did not know what to say to him.

⁴¹ Returning the third time, he said to them, "Are you still sleeping and resting? Enough! The hour has come. Look, the Son of Man is betrayed into the hands of sinners. ⁴² Rise! Let us go! Here comes my betrayer!"

ADVICE. Jesus' advice to his disciples is 'Watch and pray that you enter not into temptation.' We can easily slip up and sin. We all know what sins we like to do more than others. The devil knows these sins too and will do his utmost to get us to disobey God. We have a source of help and power that enables us to withstand temptation. This source of help is prayer. When we are being tempted, when we are feeling sin's power over us, we should pray to our Lord and Saviour to deliver us from the temptation. Jesus also left us with an example of how to tackle temptation. Jesus used God's word to defeat the devil. God has promised that he will not allow us to be tempted beyond what we can endure. (1 Corinthians 10:13)

DAY 34 MARK 14:32 –42. ONE NIGHT IN THE GARDEN.

Do you ever think that God might want you to do something too scary for you? Well, Jesus knows how you have felt.

The real horror of it all for Jesus wasn't really that he, the glorious Son of Man, pure and eternally mighty, was about to be handed over to sinful men. Nor was it the physical pain that lay ahead. It was the separation from his Father. The 'cup' is his Father's wrath that is about to be poured out against the sin that he would bear. The Father would have to turn his face away, for God cannot look upon sin. At the moment when the Father would be most proud of his willingly obedient Son he would also be at the greatest distance from him. The perfect love and union between these two was soon to be broken. For you and me. And though he dreads it with deep agony, he will do his Father's will.

Amazingly, he is not simply thinking of himself. He thinks of the disciples, with understanding of their physical and spiritual weakness.

READ THIS THEN PRAY:
"I confess my iniquity; I am troubled by my sin." Psalm 38:18

Prayer: Lord, I see what my sin does – it separates me from the Father. My love for God is so weak that I would dread physical pain more than distance from the Father. You bore my sin and shame; you bore my separation. Help me to love you faithfully. Amen.

Words: Temptation. Pages 126–130. See also Page 15.
Maps: Gethsemane (Jerusalem). Pages 142–143.

DAY 35 MARK 14:43–65

43 Just as he was speaking, Judas, one of the Twelve, appeared. With him was a crowd armed with swords and clubs, sent from the chief priests, the teachers of the law, and the elders.

44 Now the betrayer had arranged a signal with them: "The one I kiss is the man; arrest him and lead him away under guard." 45 Going at once to Jesus, Judas said, "Rabbi!" and kissed him. 46 The men seized Jesus and arrested him. 47 Then one of those standing near drew his sword and struck the servant of the high priest, cutting off his ear.

48 "Am I leading a rebellion," said Jesus, "that you have come out with swords and clubs to capture me? 49 Every day I was with you, teaching in the temple courts, and you did not arrest me. But the Scriptures must be fulfilled." 50 Then everyone deserted him and fled.

51 A young man, wearing nothing but a linen garment, was following Jesus. When they seized him, 52 he fled naked, leaving his garment behind.

53 They took Jesus to the high priest, and all the chief priests, elders and teachers of the law came together. 54 Peter followed him at a distance, right into the courtyard of the high priest. There he sat with the guards and warmed himself at the fire.

55 The chief priests and the whole Sanhedrin were looking for evidence against Jesus so that they could put him to death, but they did not find any. 56 Many testified falsely against him, but their statements did not agree.

57 Then some stood up and gave this false testimony against him: 58 "We heard him say, 'I will destroy this man-made temple and in three days will build another, not made by man.'" 59 Yet even then their testimony did not agree.

60 Then the high priest stood up before them and asked Jesus, "Are you not going to answer? What is this testimony that these men are bringing against you?" 61 But Jesus remained silent and gave no answer.

Again the high priest asked him, "Are you the Christ, the Son of the Blessed One?"

[62] "I am," said Jesus. "And you will see the Son of Man sitting at the right hand of the Mighty One and coming on the clouds of heaven."

[63] The high priest tore his clothes. "Why do we need any more witnesses?" he asked. [64] "You have heard the blasphemy. What do you think?"

They all condemned him as worthy of death. [65] Then some began to spit at him; they blindfolded him, struck him with their fists, and said, "Prophesy!" And the guards took him and beat him.

TURN OVER PAGE FOR THE DEVOTIONAL AND THINK SECTIONS.

DAY 35 MARK 14:43-65. ARRESTED AND TRIED.

When he is arrested he does not defend himself. When he is on trial he does not defend himself. In fact, what he does say before the Sanhedrin only seals his fate.

Why is he content to be led silently, like a lamb, to the slaughter?

Remember that he's been saying for weeks that this must happen. All along he has opposed the idea that his kingship is like worldly kingship. It's not about worldly power, but about heavenly gain. What the woman did with the perfume, he is about to do with his life. The Father gains glory, Christ gains glory, the Spirit gains glory. We gain forgiveness, a new life and heaven. Creation gains its freedom from the captivity to sin and all its deadly and chaotic impact. God wins!

Unless, of course, Jesus speaks up. What if he leaps to his own defence, sends a squadron of angels to blast the Sanhedrin, liberates Jerusalem from the Romans and seizes an earthly throne? Fine. He avoids the cross; but heaven, the church and all creation lose. Satan wins.

Was he weak to stay quiet? Was he a fool to walk into the trap? I don't think so. What do you think?

THE KISS. Judas knew what he was doing, 'The one I kiss arrest him.' Jesus – betrayed with a kiss by one who had professed to follow him. A sign of friendship and love was used to betray the Son of God.

THE LAMB. Look at the Passover information on Pages 140-141 as well as in the Words section: Pages 126–130. A lamb was used for the sacrifice. It had to be spotless. Jesus is the sacrifice for our sins – the perfect Son of God. There is no sin to blemish him. The sacrifice to end all sacrifices has been made. Sin has been paid for through Christ's death.

PROPHECY. Prophets were men chosen by God to give a message to the people. This message could be about what would happen in the future. The prophet Isaiah foretold about the coming Lord Jesus over 500 years before he was born. In Isaiah chapter 53 he tells us how the Saviour would take the punishment for sin without saying a word, as quietly as a lamb. This Saviour was Jesus. "Surely he took up our infirmities and carried our sorrows, yet we considered him stricken by God, smitten by him and afflicted. But he was pierced for our transgressions, he was crushed for our iniquities; the punishment that brought us peace was upon him, and by his wounds we are healed." Isaiah 53:5.

READ THIS THEN PRAY:
"But the meek will inherit the land and enjoy great peace."
Psalm 37:11

Prayer: I know in my head that it's not weak to be meek, Lord. But my self-defensive flesh and the world around me constantly tell me that meekness is for fools and losers. I would rather be a fool for Christ and gain heavenly glory than be 'wise' for the world and lose my Saviour's smile. Please help me to be meek today for the sake of the Gospel. Amen.

DAY 36 MARK 14:66–72

⁶⁶ While Peter was below in the courtyard, one of the servant girls of the high priest came by. ⁶⁷ When she saw Peter warming himself, she looked closely at him.

"You also were with that Nazarene, Jesus," she said.

⁶⁸ But he denied it. "I don't know or understand what you're talking about," he said, and went out into the entrance.

⁶⁹ When the servant girl saw him there, she said again to those standing around, "This fellow is one of them." ⁷⁰ Again he denied it.

After a little while, those standing near said to Peter, "Surely you are one of them, for you are a Galilean."

⁷¹ He began to call down curses on himself, and he swore to them, "I don't know this man you're talking about."

⁷² Immediately the cock crowed the second time. Then Peter remembered the word Jesus had spoken to him: "Before the cock crows twice you will disown me three times." And he broke down and wept.

DISCIPLESHIP. Peter was one of the twelve disciples. Jesus had chosen these men to come with him to witness God's power at work through him. Peter had heard the Son of God speak and had seen him perform miracles. Peter had been one of a special group of people. But what did it all mean now? Why did God let this happen? Why did Peter deny Jesus? Jesus let this happen because Peter had to learn his own weakness. In future years Peter would be strong with the Lord's strength. Peter would also die for Christ, but only because he was broken in the courtyard. (Luke 8:1; 9:1; 12; 18:31.)

DAY 36 MARK 14:66–72. PETER THE BROKEN MAN.

Remember: Jesus said that Peter would deny him. Peter said "Never, Lord!" Then, yesterday, we read that Peter 'followed at a distance'. Now it's crunch time for Peter.

He is scared. He is alone, distanced from Jesus and very vulnerable. A quick-eyed servant girl asks a simple question but he denies that he was with Jesus. Then he does it again.

What must have been going on in his mind? He's obviously beside himself. What Jesus had said is coming true; what he had said himself is hollow rubbish. His discipleship, his faithfulness and his brave talk – it's all collapsing around him.

The question flies at him a third time and strikes his weak heart. He calls down curses; he swears and denies that he even knows Jesus.

Immediately, as foretold, the cock crows. Poor Peter's world caves in. He is absolutely broken by his own failure to be true to Christ.

READ THIS THEN PRAY:
"This is what the Sovereign LORD, the Holy One of Israel, says: 'In repentance and rest is your salvation, in quietness and trust is your strength.'" Isaiah 30:15

Prayer: Lord, this is strange. You might let me sin – my own choice, I know, but you might let it happen so that I come to repentance. You might let me fail you and be broken so that I might learn not to trust myself but to lean on you for strength. Thank you that you always win over sin – even mine. Amen.

DAY 37 MARK 15:1–20

Very early in the morning, the chief priests, with the elders, the teachers of the law and the whole Sanhedrin, reached a decision. They bound Jesus, led him away and turned him over to Pilate.

² "Are you the king of the Jews?" asked Pilate.

"Yes, it is as you say," Jesus replied.

³ The chief priests accused him of many things. ⁴ So again Pilate asked him, "Aren't you going to answer? See how many things they are accusing you of."

⁵ But Jesus still made no reply, and Pilate was amazed.

⁶ Now it was the custom at the Feast to release a prisoner whom the people requested. ⁷ A man called Barabbas was in prison with the insurrectionists who had committed murder in the uprising. ⁸ The crowd came up and asked Pilate to do for them what he usually did.

⁹ "Do you want me to release to you the king of the Jews?" asked Pilate, ¹⁰ knowing it was out of envy that the chief priests had handed Jesus over to him. ¹¹ But the chief priests stirred up the crowd to have Pilate release Barabbas instead.

¹² "What shall I do, then, with the one you call the king of the Jews?" Pilate asked them.

¹³ "Crucify him!" they shouted.

¹⁴ "Why? What crime has he committed?" asked Pilate. But they shouted all the louder, "Crucify him!"

¹⁵ Wanting to satisfy the crowd, Pilate released Barabbas to them. He had Jesus flogged, and handed him over to be crucified.

¹⁶ The soldiers led Jesus away into the palace (that is, the Praetorium) and called together the whole company of soldiers. ¹⁷ They put a purple robe on him, then twisted together a crown of thorns and set it on him. ¹⁸ And they began to call out to him, "Hail, king of the Jews!" ¹⁹ Again and again they struck him on the head with a staff and spat on him. Falling on their knees, they paid homage to him. ²⁰ And when they had mocked him, they took off the purple robe and put his own clothes on him. Then they led him out to crucify him.

DAY 37 MARK 15:1–20. SENTENCED TO DEATH.

The Jews didn't have the right to pass the death sentence. They had to get the Romans to do that.

Once again, when Jesus speaks it makes things worse for him. Accusations rain down on him, but he refuses to get himself off the hook. Pilate is amazed but he is also weak. Pilate has no reason for passing a death sentence, except his own political self-preservation. So he sacrifices his conscience to please the careless and fickle crowd. See how easily the crowd changes its tune from 'Hosanna!' a few days ago, to 'Crucify him!' See how they turn from welcoming their King to favouring Barabbas the criminal! Never underestimate the waywardness of the mob.

It is Jesus who pays the price in the most horrific agony of humiliation, pain, hatred and vile torture.

He might ask you to walk the path he trod; to do God's will and suffer; to endure horrors for the sake of the Kingdom. If he does, you will know that he has been there too and knows what you go through.

KING OF THE JEWS. Jesus is a King. He is the King of the Jews because he is God's chosen and anointed King – and the Jews are God's chosen people.

READ THIS THEN PRAY:
"Have I not commanded you? Be strong and courageous. Do not be terrified; do not be discouraged, for the LORD your God will be with you wherever you go." Joshua 1:9

Prayer: Lord, once again I ask you to help me be brave and suffer injustice for your sake. I know that it will not be easy to be a disciple but I thank you that Jesus knows all about it and prays for me. Amen.

DAY 38 MARK 15:21−41

21 A certain man from Cyrene, Simon, the father of Alexander and Rufus, was passing by on his way in from the country, and they forced him to carry the cross. 22 They brought Jesus to the place called Golgotha (which means The Place of the Skull). 23 Then they offered him wine mixed with myrrh, but he did not take it. 24 And they crucified him. Dividing up his clothes, they cast lots to see what each would get.

25 It was the third hour when they crucified him. 26 The written notice of the charge against him read: THE KING OF THE JEWS. 27 They crucified two robbers with him, one on his right and one on his left. 29 Those who passed by hurled insults at him, shaking their heads and saying, "So! You who are going to destroy the temple and build it in three days, 30 come down from the cross and save yourself!"

31 In the same way the chief priests and the teachers of the law mocked him among themselves. "He saved others," they said, "but he can't save himself! 32 Let this Christ, this King of Israel, come down now from the cross, that we may see and believe." Those crucified with him also heaped insults on him.

33 At the sixth hour darkness came over the whole land until the ninth hour. 34 And at the ninth hour Jesus cried out in a loud voice, "Eloi, Eloi, lama sabachthani?" -which means, "My God, my God, why have you forsaken me?"

35 When some of those standing near heard this, they said, "Listen, he's calling Elijah."

36 One man ran, filled a sponge with wine vinegar, put it on a stick, and offered it to Jesus to drink. "Now leave him alone. Let's see if Elijah comes to take him down," he said.

37 With a loud cry, Jesus breathed his last.

38 The curtain of the temple was torn in two from top to bottom. 39 And when the centurion, who stood there in front of Jesus, heard his cry and saw how he died, he said, "Surely this man was the Son of God!"

40 Some women were watching from a distance. Among them were Mary Magdalene, Mary the mother of James the younger and

of Joses, and Salome. [41] In Galilee these women had followed him and cared for his needs. Many other women who had come up with him to Jerusalem were also there.

TURN OVER PAGE FOR THE DEVOTIONAL AND THINK SECTIONS.

DAY 38 MARK 15:21–41. CRUCIFIED, DEAD AND ...

Why does the curtain rip? The curtain kept people out of the Most Holy Place – the place where God's glory came down on the Day of Atonement. They had to be kept out because of their sin. Without that sin being covered by the protective blood of a sacrifice, they would die in the presence of a holy God. That curtain represented their sinful flesh – a barrier to fellowship with God. It said 'No entry.'

It was ripped open by God because the sacrifice to end all sacrifices had been finished on the cross. Now there is blood to cover all our sin. We can come into the presence of God. No-one can keep us out and no other is needed to stand between us and him. But only – and this is vital – when we trust in what Jesus did on the cross.

All our sin became his there; all his righteousness became ours. All our separation from God became his; all his fellowship with God becomes ours. All our punishment was laid on him; all his joy becomes ours. All through the cruel, glorious cross. The curtain was torn in two. The way to God is opened by the cross. Now God says, 'Come in!' Hallelujah!

CROSS SAYINGS. In the Gospels you will read seven different things that Jesus said on the cross. He said things such as 'Father forgive them for they know not what they are doing.' But later on Jesus' tone changes – he no longer calls God 'Father'. His suffering is now so great that he can no longer have that close relationship with God, even though he is God's Son. Jesus shouts in Aramaic, 'My God, my God why have you forsaken me?' God the Father has turned his face away from God the Son. The full punishment for sin is laid on Jesus. Jesus went through all this for sinners like you and me!

JESUS. This is Day 38. Not long to go now. You may know lots of things about Jesus but do you know him as your own Saviour? Has he saved you from your sins? Ask him to do this – he never turns anyone away.

 READ THIS THEN PRAY:
"Since we have confidence to enter the Most Holy Place by the blood of Jesus, [20] by a new and living way opened for us through the curtain, that is, his body, [21] and since we have a great priest over the house of God, [22] let us draw near to God with a sincere heart in full assurance of faith." Hebrews 10:19-22

Prayer: Thank you Lord for your death on the Cross. You have made it possible for those who believe in you to draw near to God. Give me a heart full of love and faith in you. Amen.

Words: Most Holy Place; Day of Atonement. Pages 126–130.
Maps: Jerusalem, Golgotha or Calvary was here. Pages 142–143.

DAY 39 MARK 15:42–47

⁴² It was the Preparation Day (that is the day before the Sabbath). So as evening approached, ⁴³ Joseph of Arimathea, a prominent member of the Council, who was himself waiting for the kingdom of God, went boldly to Pilate and asked for Jesus' body. ⁴⁴ Pilate was surprised to hear that he was already dead. Summoning the centurion, he asked him if Jesus had already died. ⁴⁵ When he learned from the centurion that it was so, he gave the body to Joseph. ⁴⁶ So Joseph bought some linen cloth, took down the body, wrapped it in the linen, and placed it in a tomb cut out of rock. Then he rolled a stone against the entrance of the tomb. ⁴⁷ Mary Magdalene and Mary the mother of Joses saw where he was laid.

REDEEMED. Jesus is described as the one who redeemed his people. If something is redeemed that means it is bought back. It is returned to the original owner. Jesus redeems those who trust in him. We are freed from sin. He paid the price to redeem us and bring us back to God by dying on the cross. He took all the punishment that was required.

ALMOST THERE. You have one more day to go until Mission Accomplished. Congratulations on getting so far. Think about the different Bible passages you have read. You will have discovered and learned so many new things. God's word always has something to teach us. We should read it prayerfully. You may be nearing the end of the 40 Days – but keep going with God's word!

Boot Camp: Crucifixion. Pages 135–141.

DAY 39 MARK 15:42–47. BURIED.

Jesus wasn't just having a rest in the tomb for two nights and three days. It was part of his three-fold work for us. Notice that Mark picks out the three parts. Crucified, dead and buried.

During the crucifixion he endured God's curse upon sin. "Christ redeemed us from the curse of the law by becoming a curse for us, for it is written: 'Cursed is everyone who is hung on a tree.'" (Galatians 3:13) By being really dead, he endured the penalty of sin. "But you must not eat from the tree of the knowledge of good and evil, for when you eat of it you will surely die." (Genesis 2:17)

The time he spent in the tomb was the time when he endured all that death meant. In the Old Testament we learn that the grave was the place where you are cut off from God, a place of darkness and silence, a place where you are totally alone and have no voice. Jesus had to go to the grave because he had to bear all the effects of sin beyond this life. He had to go all the way down, bearing all that sin does to a person, so that we won't have to. There's nothing left to suffer! Praise the Lord!

 READ THIS THEN PRAY:
"So do not fear, for I am with you; do not be dismayed, for I am your God. I will strengthen you and help you; I will uphold you with my righteous right hand." Isaiah 41:10

Prayer: Lord, it is amazing that you have done everything for me. Thank you that Jesus even went down into the grave for me. Thank you that I have nothing to fear from death, and nothing to fear from your judgement on sin, for Jesus took it all. Amen.

DAY 40 MARK 16:1-8

When the Sabbath was over, Mary Magdalene, Mary the mother of James, and Salome bought spices so that they might go to anoint Jesus' body. [2] Very early on the first day of the week, just after sunrise, they were on their way to the tomb [3] and they asked each other, "Who will roll the stone away from the entrance of the tomb?"

[4] But when they looked up, they saw that the stone, which was very large, had been rolled away. [5] As they entered the tomb, they saw a young man dressed in a white robe sitting on the right side, and they were alarmed.

[6] "Don't be alarmed," he said. "You are looking for Jesus the Nazarene, who was crucified. He has risen! He is not here. See the place where they laid him. [7] But go, tell his disciples and Peter, 'He is going ahead of you into Galilee. There you will see him, just as he told you.'"

[8] Trembling and bewildered, the women went out and fled from the tomb. They said nothing to anyone, because they were afraid.

PETER'S DENIAL. The angel tells the women to go and tell the disciples and Peter about what has happened. Peter had denied and might have thought he was no longer included. But Jesus wanted him back. To read about what happened when Jesus spoke to Peter after the resurrection read about John chapter 21.

SPICES. Spices were used in the Middle East to anoint dead bodies. When Jesus was born the Magi came to visit him with three gifts. One of those gifts was myrrh – a spice used for anointing dead bodies. Perhaps even at Jesus' birth his gifts foretold what would happen to him.

DAY 40 MARK 16:1–8. THE END AND THE BEGINNING.

The last day of our journey with Jesus is the first day of the new creation. There's new life – his. It's life that is free from the power and the penalty of sin; life that is eternal; life that can be lived in the presence of God. That's the life that we have within us if we are Christians. His life.

There's a garden where God and people have fellowship again, where the curse has been broken, where Satan's lies are overturned by the one who is the truth. It's like the Garden of Eden put right again. There's reconciliation. Peter is going to be restored to a good relationship with the one he denied.

The angel gives the good news, but the women can't take it in. They are confused and afraid because they've forgotten that Jesus said that he would rise again. But that doesn't mean that it wasn't true.

Your life in Jesus might only just be beginning; there might be lots from these past 40 days that you forget. There might be many times ahead when you too are confused and afraid. But that doesn't mean that it's not all true. Jesus Christ has lived for you, died for you and risen for you. Now, in heaven, he prays for you. And many people involved in producing these notes will be praying with him too. Walk closely with Jesus, and may God bless you wonderfully.

READ THIS THEN PRAY:
"'Go, stand in the temple courts,' he said, 'and tell the people the full message of this new life.'" Acts 5:20

Prayer: Thank you Lord that Jesus has given me new life that will last for ever. I praise you for him, and ask that you will help me to walk with him all the days of my life. Give me the opportunity to tell someone else today about your wonderful Son. Amen.

FINAL READING: MARK 16: 9–20

[9] Now when he rose early on the first day of the week, he appeared first to Mary Magdalene, from whom he had cast out seven demons. [10] She went and told those who had been with him, as they mourned and wept. [11] But when they heard that he was alive and had been seen by her, they would not believe it.

[12] After these things he appeared in another form to two of them, as they were walking into the country. [13] And they went back and told the rest, but they did not believe them.

[14] Afterward he appeared to the eleven themselves as they were reclining at table, and he rebuked them for their unbelief and hardness of heart, because they had not believed those who saw him after he had risen. [15] And he said to them, "Go into all the world and proclaim the Gospel to the whole creation. [16] Whoever believes and is baptized will be saved, but whoever does not believe will be condemned. [17] And these signs will accompany those who believe: in my name they will cast out demons; they will speak in new tongues; [18]they will pick up serpents with their hands; and if they drink any deadly poison, it will not hurt them; they will lay their hands on the sick, and they will recover."

[19] So then the Lord Jesus, after he had spoken to them, was taken up into heaven and sat down at the right hand of God. [20] And they went out and preached everywhere, while the Lord worked with them and confirmed the message by accompanying signs.

MARK 16: 9–20. AND FINALLY – YOU.

You are described in this final passage – 'Whoever believes and is baptized will be saved, but whoever does not believe will be condemned.'

Do you believe? Are you saved?

Do you believe in the Lord Jesus Christ? Have you been saved by him?

You need to answer these questions. You must pray to God for forgiveness of your sins.

 READ THIS THEN PRAY:
"For the grace of God that brings salvation has appeared to all men." Titus 2:11

Prayer: Lord Jesus, thank you for your true word. You have told me about my sin and my need for salvation. Now that I have been told these things, help me to believe them and to obey. Amen.

WORDS

Adultery; Adulterous: An adulterer cheats against their wife or husband. They disobey God's commandment, 'You shall not commit adultery.' People can cheat on God. God deserves love and worship – but many refuse to believe in him. God calls them adulterous. Just as a wife should have the love of her husband so God should have the love of the people he created.

Alabaster: A valuable substance used to make ornaments or containers such as jewellery boxes or perfume containers.

Anointed: To be anointed is when something, usually oil, is smeared or rubbed onto you. At times this act of anointing signifies that the anointed person is being set aside for a special office. Kings are anointed at coronations to show that they have authority to rule. It is an outward sign that they are the king. Jesus is God's anointed. He has the authority to rule all.

Baptise; Baptised; Baptism: Baptism is an outward sign of washing with water, in the name of the Father, Son and Holy Spirit, which tells us about the cleansing from sin by the blood of Christ and about belonging to God. In the Book of Acts we read that the Ethiopian Eunuch and the Philippian jailor and his family were baptized.

Believe: This word means to know God not just knowing about him - but actually knowing him as your personal saviour.

Blasphemies; Blasphemy: This is to speak against God or to say false things about him. Jesus was falsely accused of this because he said he was the promised Messiah. However he spoke the truth. It was in fact those who lied about him who were the blasphemers.

Church: A building that people worship God in. It is also the group of people who follow Jesus. The church of Christ is in many countries around the world. It is growing every day.

Confess: To admit to doing something wrong. We can confess our sin to God and he is faithful and just and will forgive us our sins.

Day of Atonement: See Temple.

Denarius: A coin from the currency that was being used in Roman occupied Palestine at that time.

Elect: People chosen by God for salvation from before the creation of the world. They were not chosen because they were good or because they deserved to be chosen but because of God's grace and faithfulness.

Eternity: Eternity means never having had a beginning and never having an end. This is what God is like. He is eternal. We are created by God so we aren't eternal like he is. Our lives in this world are limited by time. God created time for us. We had a beginning when we were conceived and our lives here will end when we die. Eternity has no such limits. It had no beginning and it will have no end. It is infinite. This is impossible for us to fully understand but the Bible teaches us that when we die we too will be in eternity. Our souls and resurrected bodies will live eternally in heaven or die eternally in hell. These are solemn thoughts but it is amazing that when we trust completely in what the Lord Jesus Christ has done and understand who he is we can look forward to enjoying eternity with God in heaven for ever.

Faith: Faith is a word used to describe believing in God and Jesus Christ. If you believe in Christ you belong to the Christian Faith. The Bible describes faith as being certain of what you do not see. Though we can't see God we know he is real, we know his word is true and faithful and that we can trust in the Lord Jesus Christ to save us from sin. This is Faith.

Faithful: This means that he is completely trustworthy, we can always rely on God to do the right thing, the just thing, he is perfect and holy, we can depend on him. He is faithful.

Father: God is our heavenly Father. He is everything that a Father should be. Earthly fathers fail us – but God never fails us.

Forgiven: This is when God looks on our sin and instead of punishing us as we deserve he frees us from our sin and accepts us into his family because of Christ's death on the cross.

Gentile: This was a name given to someone who was not a Jew. A Jew belongs to the Jewish people, who were also called Israelites or Hebrews. A Gentile is someone belonging to any of the other people groups or nations.

Glorify: This means to give honour and praise to someone. We should glorify God – we should show that we love him and follow him. Nothing we do or say should bring dishonour to God.

Gospel: This is another word for good news. The Gospel of Jesus Christ is good news because he has saved his people from their sins. The first four books of the new testament are specifically called Gospels – The Gospel of Matthew; Mark; Luke and John.

Grace: God's grace is generous, wonderful, amazing, free. This is what grace is – all the wonderful things that God gives us such as eternal life, freedom from sin, heaven, love, joy, peace! Everything we need and more! This is his abundant, free grace. Grace is when God gives us what we don't deserve. We deserve death and punishment but through Christ's death on the Cross God gives all those who believe in him eternal life.

Heaven: This is where those who believe in Jesus Christ as their saviour will go to when they die. God is there and he will take his people there to be with him for all eternity. The souls of believers go to be with the Lord at the moment of their death and on the Day of Judgement our risen, perfect bodies will be reunited with our souls in this glorious, sinless place.

House of God: This describes the temple where God was worshipped. We can worship God anywhere. He is not fixed to buildings.

Immorality: See Morals.

Jews: The Jews were described as God's chosen people. Today God's chosen people come from not just one tribe but from many tribes and nations and languages.

Leprosy: Today this is known as a flesh wasting disease. When we read the word leprosy in the Bible it isn't necessarily the disease we know as leprosy today. The word was used to describe a variety of skin conditions. Miriam, Moses' sister, had leprosy (Numbers 12:10) also Naaman (2 Kings 5) and King Uzziah (2 Kings 15; 2 Chronicles 26). In Bible times leprosy made you 'unclean' as the ceremonies and services in the temple were concerned. If you had leprosy you were not allowed into the temple to draw near to God. People kept away from lepers and would never touch one as it would make them 'unclean' too. Lepers were social and religious outcasts. Jesus had power over this disease and cured lepers.

Miracle: This is a word for the amazing supernatural acts that Jesus performed such as healing the sick, giving sight to the blind, feeding the five thousand and walking on the water.

Morals: These are rules that people follow in life depending on what they believe is right and wrong. Unfortunately people do not always have good morals. They may publicly do what is wrong. They may misbehave, steal and cheat. To have morals that agree with God's word is good. But it is only through trusting in Christ that you can be saved from sin allowed into heaven.

Most Holy Place: See The Temple.

Parables: This is the type of story that Jesus told. He would pick every day events or objects to explain something about God.

Some people understood the parables but some didn't. Only those whose hearts had been opened by God would understand.

Passover: This is also referred to as The Feast of Unleavened Bread: See Page 140-141.

Passover Lamb: This is the sacrifice that was offered at the Passover or The Feast of Unleavened Bread. See Page 140-141.

Praise: This is when we tell God how wonderful he is and how we are thankful for who he is and what he has done for us

Preach: This word means to tell others about the good news of Jesus Christ, to teach people about God, and to explain God's word to them. Preaching is a very important part of the life of the church.

Pure nard: A valuable perfume. Perfume and oils played an important role in biblical times. They were used at important occasions. The perfume that the woman poured on Jesus' feet could have been something that she was keeping for her wedding day. Perfumes were often kept for special days like that.

Repent: This is when someone is sorry for their sin and turns away from it. Turning to God instead to forgive them of their sins and to help them live a righteous life in the future.

Rabbi: This is a word used to describe a Jewish teacher of God's word. Jesus was referred to as Rabbi or Teacher by his followers.

Repent; Repentance: This means to turn away from your sin and turn to God. You are sorry for your sin and stop doing it. The desire to repent of sin is something that is given to you by God.

Righteous: God is righteous. To be righteous means to be like God – without sin. We can be righteous only because of Jesus. If we turn to him he will cover us with his righteousness. There is nothing in us that is righteous.

Romans: The name of the people group who were the occupying force in the region of Palestine during the life of Jesus.

Sabbath: The Sabbath was the seventh day of the week (our Saturday), the day of rest for the Jews. The Christian church has a special day of worship and rest on the first day of the week, (Sunday or the Lord's Day). This celebrates the resurrection of Jesus Christ, who rose from the dead on the first day of the week.

Salvation: This is when Jesus saves his people from their sin. It is what we receive when we repent of our sin and turn back to God.

Self-righteousness: People who are self righteous believe that they are good enough to please God and by their good works they will get into heaven. This is not true – '...all have sinned and fall short of the glory of God 'Romans 3:23 'There is no one righteous, not even one.' Romans 3:1.

Soul: God breathed into Adam (the first man) the breath of life and Adam became a living soul. You have a soul too - you aren't just a body. It will last forever – either in heaven or in hell. Our bodies will too after they are resurrected. God tells us in his word that we are to love the Lord our God with all our heart, soul and mind. Matthew 22:37.

Sovereignty: This is used to describe God's absolute power and authority over all creation, mankind and everything that happens. Nothing happens without his knowledge. He is in control. He knows what is for the best and even when bad things happen we can trust him. He is all powerful.

Synagogue: This was the local place of worship for Jews in Bible times. They would meet here to worship on the Sabbath.

The Temple: This was the place of worship in Jerusalem. People would go there to offer sacrifices to God of young lambs or pigeons. The temple was divided into different areas. One area was called The Most Holy Place. This was where the High Priest went each year to seek forgiveness from God for the sins of the people. This day was The Day of Atonement.

Temptation: This is something that prompts desire in us to do what is against God's law. Jesus knows what it is like to be tempted. He was tempted by the devil. The difference between Jesus and us is that we often give into temptation. He never did. Jesus is sinless.

Testimony: This means a story or account of facts. If you give a testimony you are telling others about something that has happened. Christians are told to give an account or testimony of how God has helped them and saved them from sin.

Transfigured: This is the word used to describe what happened to Jesus when he went up the Mountain with Peter, James and John. His whole being was lit up in a powerful and magnificent way. He was transfigured or changed brilliantly.

Worship: This is the act of praising and glorifying God. It is something that God wants us to give to him. Worship can give us joy but it should be more about what it gives to God than what it gives to us.

WHO'S WHO

FRIENDS AND FOLLOWERS OF JESUS

Disciples: The twelve men chosen by Jesus to be his special followers. Simon Peter; James son of Zebedee and John his brother; Andrew, Philip, Bartholomew, Matthew, Thomas, James son of Alphaeus, Thaddaeus, Simon the Zealot and Judas Iscariot. Judas Iscariot betrayed Jesus and was replaced by Matthias. (Acts 1.)

John the Baptist: A New Testament prophet and a cousin of Jesus Christ. His parents were Zacharias and Elizabeth. He was chosen by God to prepare the way for Jesus. He preached about the need to repent of sin and turn to God. He baptized Jesus Christ in the River Jordan. But was imprisoned and executed by King Herod.

John's Disciples: John the Baptist's followers. Some became Jesus' disciples.

Levi: See Matthew

Mark: He wrote the Gospel of Mark and was an evangelist. It is probable that he was present in the Garden of Gethsemane when Jesus was arrested. He knew the disciples well, particularly Peter. He was also involved in Paul's missionary travels and was with Paul during his final imprisonment.

Matthew: A disciple of Jesus who was a tax collector. He was also called Levi. Matthew wrote the Gospel of Matthew.

Mary Magdalene: Women were also followers of Jesus. Mary Magdalene was demon possessed but Jesus cast out seven demons from her. She was one of the first of Jesus' followers to see him risen from the dead.

Peter: One of the disciples of Jesus who worked as a fisherman. He witnessed many of Jesus' miracles. He also denied Jesus prior to the crucifixion. He was reinstated and wrote the books of 1 Peter and 2 Peter in the New Testament.

Tax Collectors: Tax Collectors collected money from the people to give to the Roman forces. The people did not think these taxes were fair so the Tax Collectors were disliked. Some Tax Collectors such as Zaccheus were also cheats (Luke 19). Jesus often ate with Tax Collectors and sinners (Matthew 9).

NAMES OF JESUS AND TITLES

Christ: See Messiah.

Jesus Christ: The Son of God, who was sent to this world as a human child within the womb of the virgin Mary. With no earthly father he was conceived with the power of the Holy Spirit.

Jesus of Nazareth: Jesus was brought up in Nazareth. Sometimes he is referred to as a Nazarene. This tells us where he came from but it has a special meaning which is set apart. In the Bible a Nazarene made special promises or vows to devote themselves to God.

Jesus Son of David: This is a description of Jesus to show that he is in the royal ancestral line of David. The fact that he is in David's family tree is one thing that proves he is the promised Messiah.

King of the Jews: A title given to the Lord Jesus Christ which shows his God given authority over God's chosen people.

Lord of the Sabbath: The Sabbath was a day of rest and for worshipping God. The title of Lord of The Sabbath means that because Jesus is the Creator he is the Lord of this special day. The Sabbath day is a day for him in that he is fully man and fully God. This day of rest was made for worshipping God and it was a gift for mankind (Mark 2:27). He made it, was Lord of it and therefore knew what was right and wrong for the Sabbath.

Messiah (Christ): Means Promised One. God promised a Saviour in the Old Testament and Jesus is the fulfilment of that promise.

Son of Man: This title belongs to Jesus Christ because as well as being fully God he is also fully human.

THE TRINITY

God the Father: This is the first person of the Trinity. Jesus Christ intercedes for his people before God the Father. He prayed to God the Father often. He prayed to God the Father specifically for those people that God the Father had given to him.

God the Son: Jesus Christ is the second person of the trinity, he is God the Son. The other two persons are God the Father and God the Holy Spirit. All three persons are one God.

God the Holy Spirit: This is the third person in the Trinity. Jesus promised that when he went back to heaven the Holy Spirit would come as a comforter. This is what happened on the Day of Pentecost - you can read about that day in the Book of Acts.

ENEMIES OF JESUS

Abiathar the High Priest: Only the High Priest was allowed into the Most Holy Place (See Words section: Temple), where he would come before God to plead for the forgiveness of the people. Abiathar was a high priest. In Jesus' time not all religious leaders truly worshipped God. They did not recognise Jesus as the Son of God.

Beelzebub: See Satan.

Caesar: The Roman Emperor. His occupying forces controlled a large area of Europe and North Africa. He was worshipped as a god by his people and controlled his provinces by the means of governors, one of whom was Pilate.

Chief Priests: Enemies of Jesus and religious leaders.

Demon: See Evil Spirits.

Devil: See Satan.

Evil spirits: These are spirits that are in league with the Devil. Jesus has power over them and we read in God's word of times when Jesus cast them out of people.

King Herod: There are two King Herod's referred to in the Bible. One was on the throne at Jesus' birth and the other at his death. Neither Herod was a descendant of King David. Jesus was brought before King Herod for questioning prior to his crucifixion. This same King Herod was responsible for the beheading of John the Baptist.

Herodians: The Herodians were the supporters of King Herod.

Pharisees: Many of Jesus' enemies were powerful, religious leaders. However, some of these people did come to believe in Jesus Christ for themselves – one such person was Nicodemus who you can read about in the Gospel of John chapter 3.

Pilate: Pilate was the Governor of Judea. Under Caesar, the Roman Emperor, Pilate was in charge of the occupying Roman forces there. Pilate, as Rome's chief representative in Judea was the only one who could ultimately send someone to execution. This is why the Jewish religious leaders approached him. Pilate knew Jesus was innocent but in the end he wanted an easy life and handed Jesus over to be crucified. Pilate's wife warned him not to touch Jesus because she had had a dream about him, Pilate paid no heed. However when the religious leaders said that the sign at the cross should say, 'He said he was the King of the Jews.' Pilate wrote, 'Here is the King of the Jews.'

Priests: Enemies of Jesus and religious leaders.

Sadducees: Enemies of Jesus and religious leaders.

Satan: Satan is the evil one, the one in opposition to the one true and Holy God. Satan also referred to as The Devil; Beelzebub.

Sanhedrin: This was a council of 71 Jewish men who were in charge of the day to day lives of the Jewish people. They were the Jewish court of law - but in Jesus' time they were under the authority of the Roman occupying forces.

Teachers of the Law: Enemies of Jesus and religious leaders.

OLD TESTAMENT CHARACTERS

Abraham: God chose Abraham to be the father of the Jewish nation. He promised him that his descendants would be like the stars - too many to count. God made a promise to him that his descendants would have a land of their own one day.

David: David is an Old Testament king. From a young age he trusted God. He wrote many songs and poems in the book of Psalms. He is in Jesus' family tree. (Matthew chapter 1.)

Elijah: Elijah is an Old Testament prophet. He performed miracles through God's power. He stood up against the wicked King Ahab.

Isaac: The son of Abraham.

Isaiah: An Old Testament prophet who was given future revelations about the coming of Jesus Christ.

Jacob: The son of Isaac.

Jeremiah: Jeremiah was an Old Testament prophet and he wrote the book of Jeremiah and Lamentations in the Old Testament.

Malachi: Malachi was an Old Testament prophet and he wrote the last book in the Old Testament.

Moses: Moses lead the Israelites out of slavery in Egypt to the land that God had promised. He was the one that God gave the ten commandments to. You can read about him in the book of Exodus.

BOOT CAMP: 001 – GETTING STARTED WITH YOU.

 WHO ARE YOU? When asked that question you'll give your name. You might add something about where you are from and what you do. Someone else has different answers. There is nobody else exactly like you. However, there are things that everybody has in common.

1. We are all human beings. God created us.

CREATED BY GOD. This means made by God. God is our Creator. He made the world. The universe and everything that exists in it - is his creation.

2. We all sin. We disobey God.

SIN. This is disobedience to God's instructions in thoughts words or deeds. If we do not listen to or obey God then we don't love him. That is sin.

3. Sin deserves God's punishment.

PUNISHMENT. The punishment for sin is death – eternal death in hell. So sin is a big problem for all of us.

Sin is failing to match the perfect standard God has set. You may think that you aren't that bad. But the Bible tells us that the soul that sins shall die and that all have sinned. We cannot get to heaven on our own. God's word tells us that if we trust in Jesus Christ we will be given eternal life. Remember that 'the wages of sin is death but the gift of God is eternal life through Jesus Christ his Son.'

HEAVEN. This is one of the places that you can go to when you die. You can only go there if you love and trust in Jesus Christ. Heaven is perfect in every way because it is where God is. There is no sin there.

HELL. Those who do not turn away from sin to follow Christ go to Hell when they die. Just as heaven is for ever so is hell.

THE DEVIL. He is in conflict with God. He tempted the first human beings. Sin, death and the Devil have been defeated by Jesus Christ and his death on the cross.

Remember that the wages of sin is death but the gift of God is eternal life. Does the fact that God is willing to give you a gift make you wonder about what God is like? Lets find out!

BOOT CAMP: 002 – GETTING STARTED WITH GOD.

 WHO IS GOD AND WHAT IS HE LIKE? Have you ever tried to describe someone when they are not there? You might describe their appearance, their likes and dislikes, how they behave, what they do. But a verbal description doesn't really show what your friend is like? To know what someone is really like you have to meet them for yourself.

Describing what God is like is difficult too. You can't see God because he is a Spirit, he doesn't have a body. Jesus Christ, also known as God the Son, does have a body. Jesus was on earth for a while, but is now in heaven. We can't physically see God the Father. We can't see God the Son either – at least not yet. So how can we know God for ourselves? What is he like? The Bible tells us some things:

1. God is faithful. Deuteronomy 7:9
2. God is love. Romans 5:8
3. God is just or fair. Psalm 9:16

There are many other things that we can find out about God in his word, The Bible.

GOD'S WORD. This is also called The Bible. It was written by different people but each of them was told what to write by God. There are two main sections – the Old Testament and the New Testament. The Old Testament teaches us about what God did before Jesus came to earth and then the New Testament teaches us about the life of Jesus and what happened after his death and resurrection.

BOOT CAMP: 003 – INTRODUCING JESUS.

 GETTING TO KNOW CHRIST! To really know someone you have to meet them and get to know them personally. You have to love them and be close to them. It is the same with God. And the only way we can really get to know God is through Jesus Christ, his Son. Jesus came to earth to bring people back to God.

CHRISTMAS. Read the REAL Christmas story for yourself in Matthew chapters 1 and 2; and Luke chapters 1-2.

Jesus was born as a human baby. So he was fully man and fully God. But though he was human like us he was sinless. Because he was sinless he was the only one who could take God's punishment for sin. This is what happened when he died on the cross. Because Jesus took this punishment from God his Father human beings can be saved from sin. When you trust in Jesus Christ, when you believe that he has taken the punishment for your sin, when you turn from your sin and give your love to God – you will be saved.

AUTHORITY. Jesus Christ has all power and authority. This has been given to him by God the Father. He has authority over creation, sickness and disease. He even has authority over death and sin. He can forgive sins. He conquered sin, death and the devil on the cross. His authority and control is over all things. The devil can do nothing that is outside God's control. He has authority over you and me. There is nothing that can separate us from his love when we trust in him. There are no leaders or powers that can thwart his plans or purposes.

BOOT CAMP: 003 — INTRODUCING JESUS.

CRUCIFIXION. This was the method of execution that the Romans used at the time of the occupation of Palestine. It is the method they used to kill Jesus. A cross was made out of wood, onto which a criminal was nailed. The criminal was then left to hang there until he died. The Jewish religious leaders falsely accused Jesus of many things and then handed him over to the Roman authorities. Pilate, the Roman governor, made a weak attempt to free Jesus but in the end he agreed to crucify him.

Note that there is more to Christ's crucifixion than a murder. Jesus had to die in order to save people from their sins. The punishment for sin had to be paid otherwise sinners would not be allowed into heaven. So although this crucifixion is a dreadful event, it is also the one event that brings sinners back to God.

RESURRECTION. The resurrection is what happened three days after the death of Jesus Christ. He was raised to life again. This shows that he had accomplished everything he had come to do. He had defeated the power of sin and death. His body was raised from the dead. All who trust in Christ will be raised to life again too, with bodies that will last forever. With these bodies we will be with Jesus for all eternity – sinless, holy and praising God.

ASCENSION. After the resurrection Jesus was seen by many people. After he had promised the disciples the gift of the Holy Spirit, Jesus went back to heaven. He ascended to heaven in a cloud. Right now he is in the presence of God the Father and he is praying for his people.

BOOT CAMP: 004 — IN THE BEGINNING.

CREATION (GENESIS 1—3). God created the world and human kind. He created everything perfectly. There was no sin. On Day 7 of creation God rested – not because he was tired, but because he was starting something special: A day of rest for mankind – The Sabbath, or The Lord's Day. The first man and woman – Adam and Eve – lived in the Garden of Eden. In the garden there were lots of fruit trees. But there was one tree that God instructed Adam and Eve not to eat from. This was the tree of knowledge, of good and evil.

THE FALL (GENESIS 3). The Devil, in the guise of a serpent, deceived Eve into eating the forbidden fruit. She ate it and then gave some to Adam. He ate it too. Sin entered the world. The world was spoiled as was Adam and Eve's relationship with God. God had to banish them from the Garden, but there was a special promise that he made. He promised to send a rescuer. One of Eve's descendants would finally destroy the Devil who had caused such harm. This descendant was Jesus Christ, the Son of God himself.

BOOT CAMP: 005 - THE OLD TESTAMENT.

 THE OLD TESTAMENT. The account of Creation and the Fall is at the beginning of the Bible in the Old Testament. Other incidents follow which explain about what happened from then on. After the flood, (Genesis 6-8), we read about the sons of Noah and the people who came after that. Abraham and Sarah were chosen by God to begin a new nation called The Israelites. God promised Abraham and his descendants that they would have a land of their own. Abraham's son was named Isaac and his son was named Jacob, Jacob had twelve sons – one of which was Joseph. Joseph's brothers sold him as a slave to Egypt. Eventually he was helped by God and rose to a high position in the land of Egypt. He was used by God to save the lives of the very brothers who had sold him into slavery. His older brother Judah is the one however who features in the family tree of the Lord Jesus.

THE EXODUS (BOOK OF EXODUS). The Israelites stay in Egypt did not work out well in the end. A new Pharaoh was crowned and he did not like the Israelite people. This Pharaoh enslaved the Israelites and they were treated harshly. The Egyptians even attempted to kill all the Israelite baby boys. One however escaped and was rescued by Pharaoh's daughter. His name was Moses. In the end God told Moses to lead his people out of Egypt to the land that he had promised them. Pharaoh would not agree to this. God sent plagues on the Egyptians. It was not until the tenth plague that Pharaoh agreed to let God's people go. The Israelites left for the Promised Land. It took them many years but God looked after them. Eventually the descendants of Abraham made it to the land God had promised.

BOOT CAMP: 005 - THE OLD TESTAMENT.

PASSOVER OR FEAST OF UNLEAVENED BREAD. The Passover was a feast that the Israelites celebrated in honour of the day that God released them from the Egyptians. The Israelites were told to have a special feast of lamb and bitter herbs and flat bread. They were to be ready to leave their homes at a moments notice. All the Israelites had to sacrifice a lamb. The blood of the lamb was to go on the doorposts of their houses and on the lintels. This would be a sign to the angel of death to pass over these houses and not to touch any who were inside. However, the angel of death visited the Egyptians. The first born in every family died. When the angel of death passed over the houses of the Israelites this was a wonderful time for them – they had been saved. God instructed them to remember this special day by having a celebration every year.

THE TEN COMMANDMENTS. When the Israelites travelled to the Promised land God instructed them how to live. He gave ten specific instructions called The Ten Commandments. These were written by God himself into two tablets of stone and given to Moses. Read about this in Exodus 20.

 MAPS

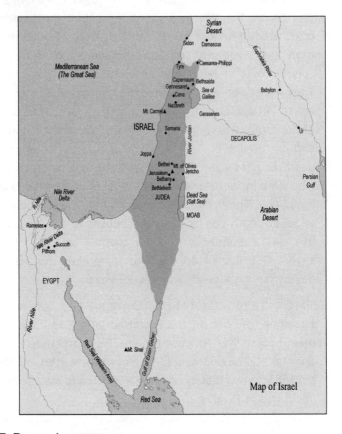

Map of Israel

40 Days: Locations

A JOURNEY THROUGH THE GOSPEL OF MARK

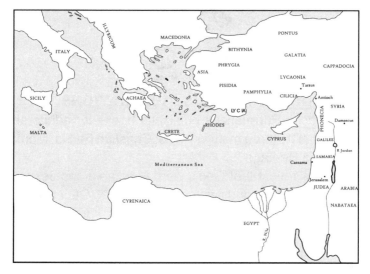

LANDS OF THE NEW TESTAMENT

River Jordan: Pages 10; 12; 26; 72; 130
Galilee: Pages 12; 16; 26; 43; 54; 67; 103; 117; 122
Sidon: Pages 26; 54.
Syria (Syrian Desert): Page 54
Tyre: Pages 26; 54.

Extra Old Testament Locations:

BABYLON: Read about Daniel in the book of Daniel.
BETHEL: Read the story of Jacob's dream in Genesis.
EGYPT; RIVER NILE; RED SEA; MT. SINAI; RIVER NILE: Read about Moses and The Ten Commandments in Exodus.
JOPPA: Read about Jonah in the book of Jonah.
MOAB: Read about Ruth the Moabitess in the book of Ruth. She was one of the ancestors of King David, and of the Lord Jesus.
MT. CARMEL: Read the story of Elijah and the Prophets of Baal in 1 Kings.
UR: Read about Abraham who came from the city of Ur in the book of Genesis.

Extra New Testament Locations:

BETHLEHEM: Read about the birth of Jesus in Matthew and Luke.
CANA: Read about Jesus' first miracle in the Gospel of John.
DAMASCUS: Read about Paul on the road to Damascus in Acts.

CHRISTIAN FOCUS PUBLICATIONS

Christian Focus Publications publishes books for adults and children under its three main imprints: Christian Focus, Mentor and Christian Heritage.

Our books reflect that God's word is reliable and Jesus is the way to know him, and live for ever with him. Our children's publication list includes a Sunday school curriculum that covers pre-school to early teens; puzzle and activity books.

We also publish personal and family devotional titles, biographies and inspirational stories that children will love. If you are looking for quality Bible teaching for children then we have an excellent range of Bible story and age specific theological books. From preschool to teenage fiction, we have it covered!

Find us at our webpage:
www.christianfocus.com

BLYTHSWOOD CARE

Blythswood Care is a Christian charity involved in care projects in south east Europe, in international aid and in the distribution of Christian literature. Since 2002, Blythswood Care has cooperated with Christian Focus Publications in the production of children's books in several European languages.

Find us at our webpage:
www.blythswood.org